THE CULTIVATION OF MUSHROOMS

By

W. F. BEWLEY, C.B.E., D.Sc. V.M.H.
Experimental and Research Station, Cheshunt, Herts
and
The late J. HARNETT
Hoddesdon, Herts

THIRD EDITION REVISED AND ENLARGED

PREFACE

In the preparation of this book we have attempted to describe in detail the various processes which must be carried out and the precautions to be taken to produce a successful commercial crop of mushrooms free from damage by diseases and pests.

It includes a working description of the recognised method of growing mushrooms on shelves in specially constructed mushroom sheds and embodies the results of research since the first issue in 1934.

The mushroom has always attracted the attention of research workers in many parts of the world because there are so many unknowns in its cultivation and growth. Despite a considerable volume of published results, it is doubtful if we have penetrated much beyond the fringe of knowledge that still remains unrevealed. In recent years, however, research has been started at many centres and we look forward to considerable progress in the not too distant future.

The authors gladly acknowledge their indebtedness to Mr. J. E. Morton, of the Experimental and Research Station, Cheshunt, for Plates X to XV and Plate XVIII, to Mr. E. R. Speyer, also of the Experimental Station, for Plates XVI and XVII, and to the late Mr. A. R. Wills of Romsey for Plate VI.

CONTENTS

CHAP.		PAGE
I.	THE MUSHROOM	9
II.	WHERE MUSHROOMS CAN BE GROWN	15
III.	THE COMPOST FOR THE CULTIVATION OF MUSHROOMS	31
IV.	THE PREPARATION, SPAWNING, AND CASING OF THE BEDS	41
V.	CARE OF THE BEDS, PICKING, GRADING, AND PACKING	58
VI.	DISEASES AND PESTS	65
VII.	COOKING RECIPES	90

CHAPTER I

THE MUSHROOM

Although a great many edible fungi grow in the fields and woods of this country, the majority are regarded with suspicion by the general public, the notable exceptions being the mushrooms which have been used for food from the earliest times. Of the wild forms *Psalliota (Agaricus) campestris*, the common or field mushroom, and *Psalliota arvensis*, the horse mushroom, are most common. The cultivated mushrooms have been evolved from these.

The flesh being white and somewhat brittle has an attractive appearance, while its delicious odour and flavour stimulates the appetite and renders the mushroom a valuable addition to the ordinary diet.

Chemical analysis has shown that the mushroom contains some 92 per cent water, 4·0 per cent protein, 0·3 per cent fat, and 3·5 per cent carbohydrates, the remaining constituents being in the form of cellulose and mineral ingredients, mainly salts of potassium and phosphorus.

Mushrooms may be cooked in a variety of ways. They may be fried in butter, boiled in milk or flour and water after previous frying, incorporated in omelets, or used for seasoning soups, sauces, ketchups, etc.

Botanically the mushroom belongs to the family of the *Agaricaceæ*. Its life cycle may be divided into three

The Cultivation of Mushrooms

parts (1) the spore, (2) the mycelium or spawn, and (3) the sporophore or mushroom. The full-grown mushroom consists of a centrally placed thick stalk or stripe, which supports the large cap or pileus, the diameter and thickness of which depends upon the variety and the conditions under which it is grown. The top surface of the cap is covered with a soft, silky, skin-like layer which usually peels off quite easily. It varies in colour from white to cream and dark brown in accordance with the variety. The under surface is composed of the lamellæ or gills which are free from the stem, rounded behind and broader in the middle. These are white at first, turning from delicate pink to dark brown and finally blackish brown as the mushroom ages.

The gills are covered with the hymenium or spore-bearing surface.

Each mushroom produces thousands of millions of brownish purple spores, which are thrown off and blown by the wind over the surface of the land. The truth of this statement can be readily observed by cutting away the stem from a fully grown mushroom and placing the cap, gills downwards, on a sheet of white paper. After twenty-four hours, in a still atmosphere, the paper will be covered with a fine brownish purple powder in a definite pattern known as the " spore print ". This is made by the spores falling vertically from the gills.

The stalk is usually white or cream with a soft core. It is encircled by a ring of tissue known as the annulus, which is a portion of the tissue which connected the periphery of the cap to the stem before the mushroom opened. When expansion occurs the tissue is torn, a fringe is left round the edge of the cap, and the annulus remains around the stalk.

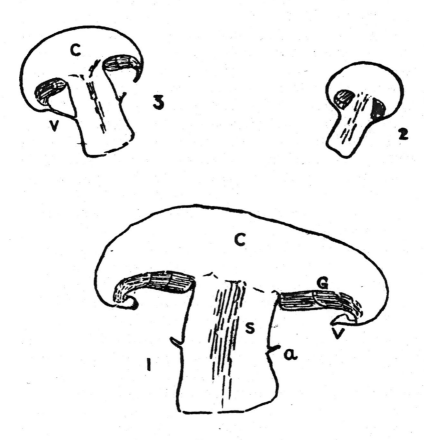

FIG. 1.

1. Mature mushroom showing remnants of the veil *v*. annulus *a*. stalk *s*. cap *c*. gills *g*,
2. Immature or " button " stage.
3. "Cup" Mushroom with veil intact *v* and broken on the opposite side.

The Cultivation of Mushrooms

In nature the spores from the mature mushroom fall to the ground amongst the decaying grass, leaves, and other organic material. Under suitable conditions they germinate and produce a dense mass of fungal threads which constitutes the mycelium or spawn. This continues to grow until the top layer of the soil is thoroughly impregnated. The fungal threads being so densely interwoven frequently unite by fusion and then produce the fruiting bodies or mushrooms. When these are first observed they appear as tiny masses of fungal threads but these soon increase in size until the " button stage " is reached. The " button " then expands rapidly and the fully developed mushroom appears.

France has been the home of mushroom culture for many generations, and it seems that French gardeners were the first to attempt it. They soon discovered that if fresh spawn taken from the fields is " planted " in heaps of suitably prepared manure it will spread rapidly through the compost and that mushrooms may be picked from the surface for a certain period.

Successful mushroom production depends upon a great many factors, but a plentiful supply of clean vigorous spawn is essential. In France " flake " spawn was most popular. This was prepared by collecting virgin spawn from the fields and growing it in special beds of animal droppings, leaf mould, and loam. When the compost was thoroughly impregnated with the greyish white growth of the spawn, it was broken down and used for spawning purposes. It was never popular in this country for it soon loses its vitality and is not easily transported.

In England " brick spawn " was used for many years. This was made by mixing cow or horse manure,

The Mushroom

sometimes both, with straw litter and a proportion of loam, and moulding the compost, while still soft, into bricks 8 × 5 × 1¼ inches. These were partially dried and inoculated by placing a small piece or more of spawn in each and then stacked together in heaps. An easier method of inoculation was to place the bricks one above the other with pieces of spawn between.

The heaps were covered with sacks or horse manure to keep them suitably moist and warm and when the bricks were impregnated with the mycelium they were taken out and dried.

The old type of brick spawn served a useful purpose in its time, and it would be unfair to criticize it unduly. Much of it was clean and vigorous, but under the conditions of manufacture it was not easy to provide adequate protection against infection by other fungi. Pure culture spawn, including the new pure culture impregnated brick spawn, is a considerable improvement upon the old spawn and is more vigorous than the old types. Prepared under proper conditions it is free from contaminations and can be relied upon to yield a much heavier crop.

In this process cultures taken direct from the mushroom are grown on sterilized media in glass bottles or other containers. If the work is properly done the final product consists of sterilized material permeated through and through with mushroom mycelium only.

The preparation of pure culture spawn cannot be done by everyone. It is a specialist's business, and mushroom growers would be wise to leave this part of the work to those who have special facilities for it.

It requires the same careful attention and clean workmanship as the preparation of fungus and bacterial

The Cultivation of Mushrooms

cultures for brewing, cheese-making, etc. Special laboratories, inoculation rooms, culture chambers, drying and storage rooms are necessary for success: without these it is impossible to guarantee a reliable product and freedom from contamination.

Many different strains of mushrooms are available to-day and spawn can be purchased to produce mushrooms of almost any shade from the most perfect white to cream, light brown, and dark brown. The colour of the mushrooms from any spawn can be altered slightly by the conditions under which they are grown. Thus mushrooms which are white in total darkness often show a slight brownish tinge when exposed to the light.

CHAPTER II

WHERE MUSHROOMS CAN BE GROWN

Although the principles underlying the successful cultivation of mushrooms on a commercial scale do not differ very greatly, the actual process may be carried out in a variety of different structures and situations. Mushrooms can be grown in any dark or semi-dark, cool building, cave, or cellar, without artificial heat, provided the temperature does not fall below 50°F. or rise above 70°F. At 50°F. or a few degrees lower the beds require covering with straw.

Many glasshouse nurserymen adapt their houses for mushroom cultivation during the period September to March, between crops of tomatoes or other glasshouse plants, and it is possible to extend the work through the summer months if special measures are taken to keep the houses cool. Mushrooms are also grown extensively in cold frames, under improvised shelters, in caves and tunnels, and on covered ridge beds out of doors. Latest developments involve the use of specially constructed mushroom sheds, containing tiers of shelves on which the beds are placed. Successful mushroom cultivation reaches its peak in such houses, because conditions can be controlled and the crops can be grown at any time of the year.

Temporary tiers of shelves may also be erected in glasshouses so that they can be dismantled easily to

The Cultivation of Mushrooms

make way for the next tomato crop. Usually there is room for a tier of two shelves at the sides of the house and one or two tiers of four shelves in the middle of the house, according to the size.

SHEDS

(1) *Old Buildings*

If an old shed is to be adapted for mushroom cultivation it should be suitably lined, preferably with flat sheets of asbestos wood leaving an air-space between the shed structure and the lining. This will afford adequate insulation and prevent the interior from becoming too hot.

Should, however, it be intended to pick mushrooms only between the months of September and May it is not necessary to go to this trouble. It would be sufficient to clean the shed thoroughly and render it rainproof. The floor should be levelled to a fairly solid surface and dusted with lime, which should be damped with water through a fine rose.

Farm and similar buildings can be used successfully for mushroom cultivation, but if artificial heat is not available one crop each year is preferable. In this way a good deal of the risk of contamination from a previous crop may be avoided.

The beds should be made from late June to July. Picking should commence in earnest in September. As soon as the weather becomes too cold, the beds should be covered with litter, preferably of barley straw. Except during the very coldest weather the mushroom crop in such buildings will often extend well into the following spring.

A.—Mushroom shed during construction showing method of arranging shelves.

B.—Outside view of mushroom sheds, showing the lean-to at the end of the house.

C.—Three mushroom sheds built into the side of a hill showing covered entrance to the top floor, from the top of the hill.

D.—Mushroom shed at Cheshunt Experimental and Research Station.

[*Facing p*

Where Mushrooms can be Grown

When the crop is finished, every portion of the spent beds must be cleared away. The building must be fumigated, the floor treated with formaldehyde, the walls lime-washed, and a perfectly clean building left for next year's crop.

The spent manure must never be used on land outside from which soil for casing the beds is to be taken at some future time.

(2) *A Mushroom Shed for Floor Beds*

This must be constructed in such a way that it can be properly ventilated and yet be tightly closed to permit satisfactory fumigation between the crops. The walls should be constructed of bricks or of breeze blocks preferably with a suitable air space. They should be cemented on the inside with a smooth finish. Alternatively they may be of wood, lined with asbestos wood.

The roof, preferably of tiles or thatch, should be of the ridge and furrow type, lined with asbestos sheets with a suitable air space behind. Seven feet is a convenient height for the eaves and 10 feet for the ridge. This allows mushrooms to be grown on shelves if desired. Some growers who confine themselves to beds on the ground prefer a height of 5 feet to the eaves.

The length should not exceed 150 feet, and 21 feet clear inside is a convenient width. This allows either four paths each 20 inches wide and three double ridge beds 4 ft. 6 in. wide, or three paths with two flat beds each 2 ft. 9 in. wide and two flat beds each 5 ft. wide.

To ensure stability it is advisable to place a number of cross ties or principals from eave to eave. Each principal is held firmly by ties from two roof purlins.

The Cultivation of Mushrooms

There must be a door at each end of the shed, so that clean, prepared compost may be taken in at one end and the old beds wheeled out through the other. In this way it is least easy to contaminate the new compost by contact with the old beds, as would certainly happen if there was only one door. Double-sized doors, 6 ft. 6 in. high by 5 to 6 feet wide, are an advantage for they facilitate the introduction of the compost and the removal of the old beds. Each should have a small door fixed inside it, for ordinary use.

Three ventilators should be fixed in each end, the centre one being over the door, and the others as high as possible, one on either side. The central ventilator should be a louver, 2 ft. 6 in. wide by 1 ft. 6 in. high. The side ventilators should be of glass, pivoted at the centre of each side. They can be shaded as and when necessary.

Adequate ventilation is particularly necessary in the ridge. This may be arranged by fixing glasshouse ventilators 6 feet apart on one side of the ridge only, or alternatively a system of louvers to be opened or closed at will. The ventilators should take three panes of 18 × 20 in. glass each and must be heavily shaded.

The sheds may be built singly, or in blocks of not more than four sheds. If bigger blocks are built it frequently happens that some of the beds, having finished bearing prematurely, have to be taken out and new ones made. This state of affairs is most undesirable for it prevents fumigation and disinfection and leads to unnecessary contamination of clean compost.

Unless the shed is so situated that a natural temperature of not less than 50° to 55°F. can be obtained during the coldest weather, it is desirable to install a hot-water heating system. Two 4 in. pipes are sufficient to heat a 21 ft. span, one being hung from the eaves and the other in a pipe hook suspended from the middle of the principal timber. See Fig. 2. The fixing of a suitable boiler and pipe system is by no means difficult or very expensive, but it is advisable for anyone contemplating the heating of a mushroom shed to consult one of the well known hot-water heating engineers.

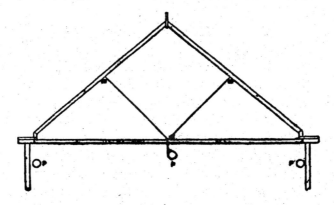

FIG. 2.—Arrangements of hot-water pipes. One centre flow and two side returns.

A cold-water supply in the shed is essential, and is best obtained by constructing a cement concrete tank in the centre. In a block of sheds it should be placed under a gutter, so that one tank serves two sheds. The inside measurements should be 6 feet long, 3 feet wide, and 3 or 4 feet deep. The tank must be kept scrupulously clean, and the top must be 2 feet above the ground level to prevent debris falling into it, and so contaminating the water. The tank is fed by a 1 in. stand pipe with a tap some

The Cultivation of Mushrooms

9 inches above the top of the tank, and so placed that a hose can be fixed for the purpose of cleaning the shed.

A concrete floor with a good smooth surface is a great advantage, for contamination of the floor occurs after a crop of mushrooms. It is also highly desirable to round off all corners.

Some form of lighting must be arranged. This can take the form of oil lamps suspended in convenient places from hooks or best of all by electric lights.

(3) *A Special Mushroom Shed*

For the mushroom specialist the type of cultivation which makes the greatest appeal and offers the maximum profit is undoubtedly that conducted with beds on tiers of shelves in a house so constructed that it can be kept sufficiently warm in winter and cool in summer. Insulation is most important because unless the internal atmosphere can be kept sufficiently cool in summer the crop suffers and insect pests become very troublesome.

Dimensions,—It is convenient to arrange two tiers of shelves on either side of a central path and provide two paths one against each wall. The shelves should not exceed 5 ft. 6 in. in width otherwise gathering of the crop is difficult. The central path should be 3 feet wide and the two outside paths should each be 2 feet wide Thus the total inside width of the house accommodating shelves 5 ft. 6 in. wide should be 18 feet. Long houses are not desirable and the best length is probably not more than 70 feet.

It is usual to build the modern mushroom shed sufficiently high to take tiers of six shelves one above the other, with a slotted floor between the third and

Where Mushrooms can be Grown

fourth shelves to divide the shed into ground floor and first floor departments (Plate IA facing p. 16). Access to the second floor is gained by means of a ladder which is usually fixed inside at the end of the shed. A better plan is to construct a " lean-to " outside the end of the house to accommodate the ladder or stairs. This acts as a wind-break and can also be used for storage purposes (Plate IB).

Should there be a hill on the nursery, it can be used to advantage so that by digging out one side the end of the shed can be built up against the hill and the first floor reached by a door to which entrance is obtained from the hill itself (Plate IIc, facing p. 17). The bottom floor is entered at ground level. Although the floor of the top storey is usually composed of battens with air spaces between, after the manner of " duck boards ", ventilation in these tall sheds is rarely satisfactory and it seems better to build lower houses to accommodate fewer shelves. Many growers have made the mistake of placing the shelves too close together for reasons of economy but the mushroom crop seems to require an ample supply of air and cramped conditions are not satisfactory.

The bottom shelf should be 12 inches above the floor to allow air to circulate beneath it and to provide room for cleaning. Two feet six inches should be allowed between the bottom of one shelf to the bottom of the next one above it, and 3 feet to 3 ft. 6 in. between the top shelf and the ceiling.

The best arrangement seems to be three shelves in a total height of 9 to 10 feet between floor and ceiling. A photograph of such a shed erected at the Cheshunt Research Station is shown in Plate IID, and it will be

The Cultivation of Mushrooms

seen that a small lean-to shed has been erected against the north end. This serves as a packing shed and also helps to keep the wind away from the north door. Entrance normally is through a door placed in the west side of the lean-to, but two large doors will be seen on the north side also. These are used when the shed is being refilled with compost: they allow the wheel-barrows to be run straight into the larger shed.

Construction.—The walls on brick or concrete foundations should be constructed with an air space for insulation purposes. The outside is usually made of feather-edged boards, overlapped to throw off the rain, and must be treated with paint or a preservative, such as Solignum, to prevent decay. They should be white, but seldom are, to reflect the sun during hot weather. The air space should be 4 inches wide and the inner lining is best constructed of asbestos wood, which can be closely fitted and which absorbs moisture without distortion and prevents sweating. Asbestos sheets are unsatisfactory for they are easily broken by contact with feet, tools, etc. Closely fitting tongued and grooved boards are most generally used, but they may absorb moisture, swell and warp badly unless treated with some suitable water-proofing material which so far has not been discovered. Suitable insulating material is expensive. Powdered cork and slabs of cork come into this category, while wood wool is unsatisfactory unless it is packed in a dry condition and kept dry.

The most recent development is the use of thin sheets of aluminium foil suspended midway between the outer wall and the lining, as a central thin partition. A high degree of insulation is claimed for this material

Where Mushrooms can be Grown

and it is worth consideration by anyone erecting new sheds. The ceiling must have a gradual slope towards the walls to allow any condensation to run down the walls instead of dripping on to the beds. It can be made of asbestos sheets or preferably asbestos wood. The wooden battens used for joining the sheets of asbestos must not be fixed parallel to the walls because in this position they will impede the flow of condensation water towards the walls. A good deal of the condensation on the ceiling can be prevented by resting sheets of some insulating material in the roof space above the celing. That part of the ceiling which comes above the central path should be flat and be fitted with ventilators the width of the flat ceiling. These should be hinged so that they open alternately in opposite directions. The opening can be facilitated by fastening a chain from each ventilator, taking it over a pulley in the roof and bringing it downwards through a small hole in the ceiling.

Above the ceiling is the roof with continuous ventilation in the ridge, produced by a system of louvers. It is a good plan to place a block in the louver channel at every 10 feet to lead the air straight out and so prevent it from accumulating at one end.

The roof is usually formed of asbestos tiles or sheets. Rubber-treated felt or similar material is often used. It is relatively cheap but becomes very hot in summer and is not really suitable.

Insulation of the roof is most important, and it should be constructed with an air space as in the case of the walls.

The shed must be fitted, if possible, with a door at each end so that clean compost can be brought in at

The Cultivation of Mushrooms

one door and the old beds removed from the other. This cannot be done where the sheds are built against a hill. Over each door should be fixed a glass fanlight to be opened for ventilation if required.

Windows can be fitted in the walls. They are useful to provide light when emptying and filling the shelves, but must be provided with shutters which are closed for the greater part of the time.

Bottom ventilation is a necessity because the air must be well circulated to prevent any undue accumulation of carbon-dioxide around the bottom beds. This can be achieved by introducing ducts through the walls immediately above the floor. These should be placed at intervals of 10 feet and should have internal measurements 18 inches by 3 inches. It is convenient to lead them into brick or wooden chambers outside the house, and these can be provided with covers to exclude the rain and regulate the in-flow of air. To ensure that the air immediately above the floor is circulated, a flat piece of wood or other material is laid over the piping on the inside of the duct to conduct the air under the bottom shelves and towards the centre of the house. In this way the cold air is passed over a hot water pipe and warmed before coming in contact with the shelves.

An air-conditioning plant would be ideal for mushroom work but the apparatus is expensive at the present time and until cheaper methods can be devised the above system of bottom ventilation is a great help especially if assisted by fans in the roof for use during hot weather.

The floor of the shed should be concreted and finished off smoothly. This assists in maintaining clean conditions and is practically a necessity. A floor of earth is undesirable for insects breed in it and form an endless source of trouble.

The woodwork erected to hold the shelves consists of a series of uprights 4 inches by 2 inches, placed 4 feet apart on either side of the shelves. These are joined

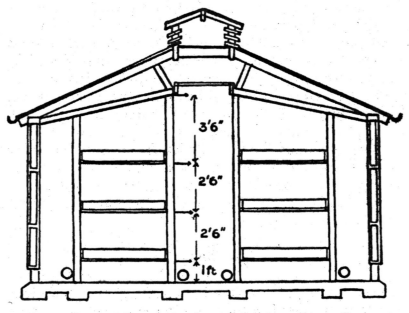

FIG. 3.—Diagram showing construction of a small mushroom shed.

together underneath each shelf by cross pieces of the same size timber bolted securely to them. These uprights are placed in position before the floor is concreted and so are held securely at the bottom. The shelves are formed by laying down boards 6–7 inches wide and 1¼ inches thick, fitting them loosely together leaving about ½ in. space between each board. The side and end boards are 7 inches by 1¼ inches, the former fit inside the uprights and are held firmly between them and the material of which the beds are composed.

All the timber comprising uprights, cross pieces, and bed boards should be of western red cedar if possible, because this timber is practically everlasting.

The heating system for a mushroom shed offers no difficulty. In a house 18 feet wide inside there should be two flows of 3 in. hot water pipes, one along the inside of each wall, and these should be continued as returns on either side of the central path at floor level. In the case of sheds with six or more shelves per tier, 4 in. pipes should be used.

Each shed must have its cold water supply terminating in a stand-pipe at the end of a short house (50 feet long), or have one at each end of a longer house.

A diagram illustrating the construction of a typical shed is given in Fig. 3.

(4) *Glasshouses*

Glasshouses can be used successfully if precautions are taken to provide adequate shading. This can take the form of whitening and oil; clay and oil; or flour, water, and brown umber applied directly on the glass; or may be material such as hessian or mats fixed to the woodwork.

This type of shading is not sufficient in really hot sunny weather, when hessian, straw, or reed mats must be fastened inside the house also. In a tomato house mats are laid over the wires across the top of the house, so as to form a flat ceiling with a narrow space in the

Where Mushrooms can be Grown

centre to allow ventilation. At the sides they are fixed to the bars by means of cardboard washers and felt nails, which are also used for lining cucumber houses, where the ceiling portion is omitted. Lengths of hessian can be fixed in a similar manner.

Exceptionally cool conditions in the hottest weather can be obtained by fixing mats as described above to the inside of the house, and also on the outside. The latter is easily done by laying the mats over the roof and nailing builder's laths along the bars with felt nails to keep the mats in postion. Care must be taken not to injure the bars.

The use of hessian within the house is an advantage,

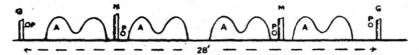

Fig. 4.—Four double small ridge beds A in a 28 ft. wide house G, gutter posts; M, purlin posts; P, pipes.

for by spraying it regularly with water during hot weather the air can be kept suitably moist and cool. Alternatively the beds can be littered with 4–6 in. straw instead of shading the house. This practice is not so good but it is necessary in winter if artificial heating is not available. The type of bed which is employed depends to a great extent upon the position of the pipes.

It is permissible to construct a flat bed across the whole house, missing the pipes. In this case it is usual to lay boards on the beds from which to do the picking and any necessary work. These may be 6 in. boards 1½ inches thick supported on two flat bricks every 2 feet. Each brick will be 2⅝ inches thick, and as the bottom one will sink into the bed, the board will stand

The Cultivation of Mushrooms

2⅝ inches above the surface and allow room for mushrooms to develop underneath.

This, however, is additional capital outlay which can be avoided by thoughtful arrangement of the beds.

Fig. 4 shows a typical tomato house, 28 feet wide with four rows of pipes, and Figs. 5 and 6 a cucumber house 14 feet wide, with a suggested arrangement of beds which has proved very satisfactory.

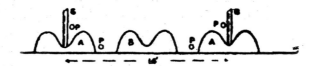

FIG. 5.—One double small ridge bed B and two half beds A in a 14 ft. wide house. G, gutter posts; P, pipes.

FIG. 6.—As in Fig. 4, but centre bed made of 8 inches of manure over a central core of old cucumber beds.

In cucumber work the old beds are frequently steamed for the following season, and when a mushroom crop intervenes, sufficient of the old cucumber beds for next season's use may be thrown into the centre of the path in a suitably shaped heap and covered with an 8 inch layer of mushroom compost which can be spawned in the usual manner. When the mushroom crop is finished most of the exhausted mushroom beds are removed. The old cucumber beds are steamed and used for making new cucumber beds at the sides in the approved manner. It would of course be necessary to clean the house thoroughly after the cucumber crop and destroy woodlice, etc., before preparing for the mushrooms.

Where, owing to force of circumstances, the pipes come very near to the bed it is advisable to cover them at such places with very thick insulation such as whole newspapers, which will be taken off and burnt when the crop is finished.

(5) *Frames*

Mushrooms can be grown in frames. The walls should be constructed of brick or built of turves laid one on top of the other. They should be covered with shaded lights or wooden lids (preferably double, or covered with straw mats). A convenient depth of frame is 18 inches to 2 feet.

The question as to whether the frames should be sunk in the ground or placed on the top, depends upon the type of soil. A sunken frame keeps warmer in winter and is cooler in summer than a raised frame, but if there is any possibility of water soaking through the sides, the frames must be placed on the surface.

(6) *Caves and Tunnels*

These are admirable situations for mushroom work, provided they can be thoroughly cleaned after each crop and are capable of being ventilated efficiently.

Usually ventilation is inadequate with the result that the carbon-dioxide produced by the crops accumulates unduly and reduces the yield. Further, in large caves

The Cultivation of Mushrooms

and tunnels fumigation is difficult because they require large quantities of gas and it is not easy to remove the poisonous vapours when they have done their work. Contamination of the floor is common and has been the cause of serious failures in the past.

With induced ventilation, the installation of suitable heating apparatus where necessary and the provision of at least one shelf, to lift the beds above the floor, successful mushroom cultivation is possible in these situations.

(7) Ridge Beds

The preparation and management of ridge beds in the open is not learned in a short time. It requires the greatest attention to details. Ridge beds are usually made with a view to cropping from late February until June and from September until the weather becomes too cold.

Since the advent of pure culture spawn, which will continue to develop at relatively high temperatures, it has been possible to continue the cropping period through the summer, except in very hot weather when special arrangements must be made to keep the beds cool.

Ridge beds are usually 2 ft. 6 in. wide at the base, tapering to a width of 6 inches at the top. The height is usually 2 ft. 6 in. (See Plate VIII facing p. 49). They can be made with or without a central core of soil which is usually 12 inches deep and 12 inches wide at the base. A core of soil is often put into the beds made in July and August (picking September and October) otherwise the beds may dry out. Those made from September until late January require more heating material and are made without a soil core.

CHAPTER III

THE COMPOST FOR THE CULTIVATION OF MUSHROOMS

Although the mushroom grows freely in widely different types of grassland, and despite the extended efforts of scientific investigators no better form of compost has been discovered for commercial work than that prepared by the fermentation of clean straw and horse manure. Well fed horses, in the diet of which corn and cake have been included, yield the most suitable manure and the material used for bedding should preferably be wheat straw. One ton of good horse manure is sufficient to make 7-8 square yards of flat bed 8 inches thick.

The manure must be comparatively fresh and generally speaking it is inadvisable to accept manure which has been exposed to the weather for any considerable period. Should the manure come from more than one source, consignments of different ages must not be mixed together.

The ideal finished product is nut-brown in colour, free from any disagreeable odour, somewhat springy, and when squeezed in the hand does not exude moisture through the fingers but leaves a dampness on the inside of the hands. The smell of the compost resembles that of mushrooms themselves. When a portion is taken in the fingers of two hands and submitted to a pulling strain it snaps cleanly and offers only a slight resistance to the pressure exerted. To reach this state the original manure must be submitted to fermentation of a very definite kind.

If the fermentation is too rapid the manure is said to burn which means that the organic portion is rapidly oxidized and what would constitute valuable food for the mushroom fungus is lost, and the compost rendered more or less unsuitable in accordance with the degree of burning.

This type of fermentation takes place when the manure contains too much straw, when the straw is too loose in the heap, is too dry, and when the weather is hot. With manure in this condition a shorter interval should be allowed between the turnings.

If, on the other hand, fermentation is too slow certain compounds which retard the development of the mushroom mycelium remain unchanged and the compost is unsuitable for mushroom growth. This occurs when the manure has been exposed to the weather for too long a period and is not sufficiently fresh; when it does not contain sufficient strawy material; when the heap is too tight and too wet; and when the temperature of the air is low.

It will be seen, therefore, that successful fermentation upon which depends the success of mushroom culture follows to a large extent the use of the right manure mixture fermented under favourable physical conditions.

It is extremely difficult to describe in words all the details of this work but the following suggestions should explain the chief features.

(1) In dry hot weather a greater proportion of fæces and less strawy material are required than in cold damp weather.

PLATE III.

Preparing the Manure.

[*Facing p.* 32

The Compost for Cultivation of Mushrooms

(2) In hot weather the manure should be damper and tighter in the heap to start with than in wet weather.

(3) During the summer the rate of fermentation can be reduced by adding a small proportion of cow manure but this should never exceed 5 to 10 per cent of the bulk and should of course be well broken up and mixed with the entire heap.

(4) During the winter when fermentation tends to be slow, it is necessary to use fresher manure than in the summer, and it must contain a greater proportion of straw.

MAKING

Under what might be termed normal conditions, which are neither too hot and dry nor too cold and wet, the manure is handled as follows:—

Normally during the summer time it is possible to do without sheds, but during the autumn and winter months some form of cover is advisable, for if the manure becomes wet to an appreciable degree through exposure to the weather, it becomes more or less useless. Most glasshouse growers commence to prepare for mushroom work as their earliest crops finish, namely from August onwards, and therefore they must make some provision for covering. If the weather is good the first two turnings can be carried out outside on a convenient site in the neighbourhood of the houses, so that the heap can be rushed inside if the weather changes. The site on which the manure is stacked must be raised a few inches above the level of the surrounding ground to prevent water draining on to it. If the heap has to be taken into the house, the ventilators must be left fully open, otherwise the water vapour which is liberated will condense on the roof and falling on the manure will make it too wet.

If glasshouses are not available a high, open sided shed must be constructed, preferably one made with iron supports and galvanized iron roof such as is used on the farm for storing hay. The dimensions can be arranged to suit individual circumstances. A concrete floor is not essential but it must be clean and a little higher than the surrounding land.

It is becoming increasingly more difficult to obtain an adequate supply of good horse manure for horticultural work and as only the very best is suitable for mushrooms the need for scientific research in mushroom composts is considerable. Until more knowledge is available the grower must be content to take the best he can procure and prepare from it the best compost it will produce.

Careful examination of each load of manure when it is being stacked for the first time is essential. Any excessively wet and evil smelling portions and all foreign material must be discarded without regret. They can be used for other purposes but are dangerous in mushroom beds.

Having cleaned up the new material the grower must next decide if straw must be added to it and if so in what quantity.

In the case of very short manure one ton of straw can be added for every 10–12 tons of manure, but less than this is usually adequate. The straw must be thoroughly soaked with water before attempting to mix it with the manure. The best method of achieving this is to immerse the bales in water in a tank, placing other bales

The Compost for Cultivation of Mushrooms

on top to prevent the lower bales from floating. In this way they will absorb about twice their weight of water.

In the absence of tanks the straw should be spread out in a thin layer and exposed to the action of a sprinkler until thoroughly wetted.

In stacking the manure at the commencement of the operations every care should be taken to make the correct type of mixture, for upon this the final product depends.

As the manure is collected it should be placed in heaps not more than 4 ft. 6 in. high in the summer and even lower if it is of a type which will heat very freely. In winter it may be 5 feet high. The size of the heap depends upon the time taken to collect it, and to secure uniformity any one heap should be collected in not more than ten to fourteen days. Later imports should be put into another heap until another ten or fourteen days have elapsed and so on.

To facilitate thorough mixing when the time for turning comes it is best to make the heap as shown in the following diagram.

15 ft.

	1st day	2nd day	3rd day
	4th day	5th day	6th day
	7th day	8th day	9th day

B ← top, A ← bottom, C upper right, D lower right, E right

It is an advantage to cover the top of the heap with two or three inches of clean loam. This helps to absorb the excess of ammonia liberated from the manure.

While collecting the manure into the first heap a light

The Cultivation of Mushrooms

treading is advisable if the material contains an undue proportion of straw. If the straw looks as if it is not thoroughly saturated with urine and seems to be on the dry side, it should be watered through a fine rose but not to such an extent that the water will run through the heap on to the surrounding ground. This, however, only applies to material collected in the summer, and if a mistake is made it is better to err on the side of dryness, rather than make the material too wet. The previous remarks with regard to the addition of new cow manure in the summer should be applied at this stage if necessary. In forming the heap it is essential to keep the sides as upright as possible, on the principle which governs the formation of a hay stack.

Assuming the heap has taken ten days to collect, it should stand untouched for approximately another ten days, during which time the temperature will have risen to between 150° F. and 160° F.

In making the first real turn two men should stand each at two adjacent corners (see Plate III facing p. 32) and fork the manure from the corner nearest them (C and D in diagram on page 35) on to the vacant ground opposite the middle of the side (E in diagram) and gradually work towards each other. As one portion is cleared, they pass on until the whole heap is turned, and their object should be to mix the outside of the heap with the inside and the material first collected with the later portions. This can only be done as shown in the diagram, by working across the narrow way of the heap. This is the correct time at which to apply water during the process of preparation, because it is the crucial stage in fermentation.

If the temperature of the heap before turning is

The Compost for Cultivation of Mushrooms

not less than 140° F., it means that the correct mixture of materials was achieved in stacking the heap and that everything is proceeding satisfactorily. Under these condtions the heap must be watered during the first real turning. The quantity to be applied must now be determined by (1) the actual dryness of the compost, (2) humidity of the atmosphere, and (3) the stage to which fermentation has proceeded.

It must be borne in mind that during the summer water is constantly lost into the atmosphere, but as the year advances there comes a time usually about late September when it almost seems as if the manure absorbs water from the air. This means than any application of water after late September must be less than that given under drier atmospheric conditions.

The safest method of watering is by means of a can, but this is a tedious operation for commercial places and it can be done by means of a ¾ or 1 in. hose to which a fine rose is fitted. When water is given it must not under any circumstances be in such quantity that it will run away from the bottom of the heap.

When at the commencement the men have turned sufficient manure to make a mound 2 ft. 6 in. high it is watered, because the outside of the heap is usually driest. It is then turned upside-down and watered again. This gives the necessary start and afterwards it is sufficient to water each fresh surface as the heap progresses, and each 6 or 9 in. layer is added.

During turning, sufficient room must be kept between the new heap and the old one to enable the floor to be kept clean all the time. This is essential to clean work.

The manner in which the manure is turned is most important. The workman takes a forkful of manure

The Cultivation of Mushrooms

and with a twisting movement shakes it out on to the new heap and in so doing the individual strands loosen and fall lightly. *During this process care must be taken to break up all big lumps*, If this is not done the centres of these lumps do not undergo satisfactory fermentation and may carry pests into the finished beds.

It is also necessary in all turning operations to see that the outside of the heap is moved to the centre and vice versa. The reason for this will be apparent at once. The twisting movement is essential for it is the only way of separating the individual strands and obtaining the correct physical conditions for further fermentation. At the end of each day's work a wooden stake is placed in each side of the heap and on it should be written the date and number of the turn.

The turned heap with upright sides may remain untouched for four clear days. This means that should the first turn be completed on Friday afternoon, the heap will be ready to turn first thing on Wednesday morning. Naturally this period need not be measured accurately to within a few hours. Should the heap not reach a temperature of 150° F. at the first turning it may be left for six or seven days before the second turning.

Ideally, all the water necessary should have been given during the first real turn, but it is almost impossible always to judge the water requirements accurately and on the second turn if there are any dry places in the heap they should be watered *lightly*, Sometimes whitish areas, "fire-fang," may appear to be dry when they are actually moist. This should not mislead the grower, who should test the compost by rubbing it through the hands.

The Compost for Cultivation of Mushrooms

Turning for the second time is exactly as before. The manure must be thrown over with the twisting movement and the sides of the heap must be left upright.

It is nearly always necessary to give three real turnings and very often a fourth may be required if the compost has not reached the condition described on page 31. Three clear days are left between the second and the third turning, unless when turning for the second time the compost appears to be reaching the ideal condition of dryness, when only two days are allowed before the third turn.

The above operations should have been carried out under a suitable shed, except in the case of glasshouse growers with no shed available. Here the first two turnings would take place outside, except in rainy weather, but the third turn or perhaps the fourth, if necessary, would have been done in the glasshouses where the beds are to be made, because rain falling on the heaps after the second turn would have a serious effect on the compost.

If, in spite of all precautions and care the compost appears to be too wet or is not sweet and a fourth turning is necessary this should be done in the house or shed where the beds are to be made. The bed should again be turned inside-out but instead of remaining in one large square or rectangular heap, it should be formed into a series of ridges about 6 feet wide at the bottom, 3 feet at the top, and 4 ft. 6 in. high. After two to three days in this position it should be ready for bed making. Alternatively the fourth turning can be avoided by mixing a little clean loam with the compost. This seems to absorb the excess of ammonia and remove the unpleasant smell. The compost can be placed loosely in the positions where the beds are required. It will dry sufficiently in two or three days to enable it to be compressed to suitable bed formation.

It was shown by Pizer[1] at Wye Agricultural College that the old practice of adding gypsum to heaps of farmyard manure could be applied with good results to the preparation of mushroom compost, and the results of his investigations have been of considerable benefit to mushroom growers. At Cheshunt 1 cwt. of gypsum is used to every 3 tons of compost, sprinkling it evenly as turning proceeds, to mix it uniformly through the heap. Where the manure obviously requires amelioration at the commencement, the gypsum is added at the first turn, but the need may not be apparent at this stage, and results suggest that it can be added as late as the fourth turn. Experiments at Cheshunt have shown that earlier and heavier crops can be obtained by adding 28 lb. of cotton-seed or castor meal per ton of manure at the first turning.

[1] *Gard, Chron.*, 100, p. 112, Aug. 1936.

PLATE IV.

MAKING A FLAT BED.

[*Facing p.* 40

PLATE V.

MAKING DOUBLE RIDGE BEDS.

PLATE VI.

RIDGE BEDS IN THE OPEN.

CHAPTER IV

THE PREPARATION, SPAWNING, AND CASING OF THE BEDS

BED MAKING

The three types of beds which are recommended for general use are the flat bed, the double small ridge bed, and the large single ridge bed, the last of which is mainly for use out of doors, or in unheated sheds.

The Flat Bed

This is frequently called the 8 in. flat bed, because of its depth when completed and before casing (Plate IV). Actually the depth varies with prevailing conditions. In a heated shed or house the depth is 8 to 9 inches, and in an unheated shed it is 8 to 9 inches in the summer and 12 inches in the winter.

Before laying the compost the beds should be lined out. String is unsuitable because it becomes entangled in the fork. The best plan is to obtain a supply of 1 in. diameter gas pipe in lengths of 12 feet. These are laid down in position on the floor of the house and fixed with iron pegs, inserted on the path side every 4 feet. A 12 ft. run of bed requires two lengths, one on either side of the bed. When the work is completed a further 12 ft. run is marked out with two similar lengths and by leaving the first two pieces in position a

The Cultivation of Mushrooms

continuous straight line can be maintained. The top of the beds is kept at a uniform height by means of stakes. For an 8 in. flat bed these are about 18 inches long with a notch cut out in the side 2 inches and 10 inches from the end. The stakes are driven into the ground up to the 2 in. notch every 4 feet down the centre of the bed. All is now ready for laying down the compost, and this is shaken down in the space between the two pieces of iron barrel, and compressed uniformly by treading. In spreading the compost the same twisting movement used in turning must be employed. For a bed 8 inches deep it is an easy matter to guage the depth of compost (about 4 inches) which will almost tread down to an 8 in. layer, and all that is required is to add a final thin layer to complete the operation. All hollow places in the surface must be filled up, and flattened with the back of a fork. The sides should be left with only the slightest slope and the bed knocked into final shape with the back of a fork. It is best to arrange two separate treadings for deeper flat beds. When treading it should be remembered that a springy compost requires more pressure than one which is dense or on the wet side.

Double Small Ridge Bed

This type of bed is 4 ft. 6 in. wide at the base and is made in three stages. Plate V and Fig. 7.

First a flat bed is marked out 4 ft. 6 in. wide and after suitable treading should finish 6 inches deep.

On this bed are two small ridges each 21 inches wide at the base and 15 inches deep from the top of the ridge to the top of the 6 in. bed, making the top

Preparation, Spawning, and Casing

of the ridge 21 inches from the ground. Two of these beds each 21 inches wide should leave a 12 in. space between, but it is usually rather less than this for the compost tends to spread when the ridges and casing are completed. Stakes are used as in the case of flat beds, but should be about 25 inches long, with notches to mark the top of the 6 in. base bed and the top of the finished ridge. Each small ridge is made in two parts on top of the base bed. First a layer of compost

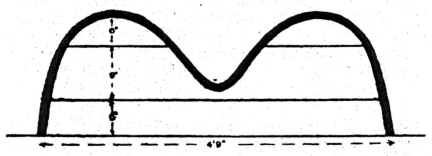

Fig. 7.—Double small ridge bed.

is trodden to about 9 inches or pressed only should the compost be rather dense, and then the cap is put on. Finally the whole of the outside is nicely moulded, by filling up the irregularities, and pressed smooth with the back of a fork.

This type of bed is very economical for it gives a large surface area.

Flat Beds on Shelves in Special Mushroom Sheds

When the shed has been thoroughly cleaned and disinfected in readiness for filling, the boards which form the shelves have been taken up and packed at one

The Cultivation of Mushrooms

side of their respective shelves. When all is ready for bringing in the compost the boards are laid down to form the two bottom shelves on either side of the path. One man stands on each shelf, after disinfecting his boots with formaldehyde, and taking the manure as it is tipped on to the shelf by other workers who bring it in barrows to the shed he works it into position without any attempt at compacting it. As the finished bed will be 7 to 8 inches deep the loose compost is filled in to a depth of 14 inches using a marked stick as a guide. When both bottom shelves have been filled up, the boards are put down to form the next shelf above and the workers climb up and stand on these in readiness to take the compost. By constructing an inclined plane of boards up to and away from the workers the compost can be run up on barrows, and tipped on to the second shelves, the workers continuing on down the slope and out at the other door. When these shelves have been filled the third shelves are put down and the compost is carried in baskets on the shoulders of the men and tipped on to the shelves, to be shaped into position as in the case of the lower shelves. A sufficient number of men must be employed as will fill all the shelves in the shed in one day.

It is of course more convenient to employ the simple conveyors which are so useful in horticultural work. The type which consists of short metal rollers mounted cross-wise in long metal frames is most convenient. It can be worked either by gravity or power.

As the filling is in progress the boilers are lighted and by the time the shed is finished the water in the pipes is nicely warm. Doors are closed, but during the first night sufficient ventilation is allowed in the roof as will

Preparation, Spawning, and Casing

carry away the water vapour arising from the compost as the house temperature rises. If the compost is a little on the wet side this drying may continue until the morning after the second night. At this point the ventilators are closed and the temperature allowed to rise for the final curing of the manure. As the shed temperature reaches 90° F., the temperature of the compost will increase to between 130° and 140° F., and when it remains constant for 24 hours " peak temperature " has been reached and the time has come for fumigation to destroy insects driven out from the compost by the rise in temperatures.

For this purpose sodium cyanide at four times the normal concentration, namely 1 oz. per 1,000 cubic feet, with the necessary sulphuric acid, or calcium cyanide, 1 oz. per 1,000 cubic feet, is employed, the shed being closed down until the next morning. It is then opened up to allow the poisonous gases to escape and fresh air to enter from outside.

At this stage the loose beds are pressed down to a depth of 8 inches and then the beds are allowed to cool, sufficient ventilation being given to prevent undue formation of condensation water on the ceiling, etc. Should condensed water drip on to the top beds they should be protected by covering them with double sheets of newspaper.

When the beds have cooled sufficiently they are spawned.

Ridge Beds in the Open

The cultivation of mushrooms on ridge beds in the field should be a profitable business for farmers, market

The Cultivation of Mushrooms

gardeners, and fruit growers. The prospective grower, however, would be well advised either to engage a practical mushroom grower to supervise the work or else undergo a course of instruction on a mushroom farm.

The area of land devoted to this work should be marked out in sites for the beds and paths, allowing a width of 3 feet for each bed (slightly more than the width of the bed itself) and 2 ft. 6 in. for the paths. The top 4 inches of soil should be skimmed off the path and placed on the adjoining bed site to make a foundation for the bed. It is an advantage to apply a light dusting of slaked lime before skimming off the soil from the paths. As soon as possible after the beds have been made the soil should be dug out of the paths and wheeled away to convenient sites for conversion into soil for casing the beds. Usually a strip of 18 inches wide and 8 inches deep, taken from the middle of the path, is sufficient.

When the crop is finished the "spent" beds can be spread over the land for future crops and the next mushroom crop taken on an adjoining site.

The advantages of this method are:—

(a) No expense is incurred in transferring soil from distant land.

(b) Water is prevented from lying at the bottom of the beds during wet weather, by the fact that the paths have been lowered by removal of the casing soil.

(c) The site receives sufficient manure from the old beds to satisfy the needs of many succeeding crops.

(d) By changing the site each time, risk of contamination from previous mushroom crops is prevented. This is one of the causes of mushroom failure.

It is best to prepare the manure under open-sided

Preparation, Spawning, and Casing

sheds and transfer it to the site. Also provision must be made for watering the beds. This can be arranged by placing galvanized iron tanks each holding 50 gallons of water at suitable intervals in the field, and filling them from a central water main. The amount of water required is not great and a 1 in. pipe is sufficient for a large area.

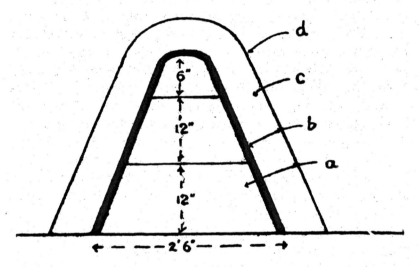

Fig. 8.—Ridge bed for the open. *a*, manure; *b*. casing, 1-1½ inch; *c*. straw, 6 inches; *d*. canvas covering.

Large ridge beds, Fig. 8 and Plate VI (page 41) are chiefly used for field work. They are 2 ft. 6 in. wide at the base and 6 inches wide at the top, which is 2 ft. 7 in. above the ground.

When they are made at the beginning of July (picking in September and October) and until the end of August they should contain a central core of soil, 12 inches wide and 12 inches high. This helps to reduce the heat in the centre and reduces the cost of manure. From the beginning of September until the end of January the central core of soil should be omitted because of the lower temperatures.

These ridges are made in three portions 12, 12 and 6 inches deep when trodden into position; the top portion being pressed down as in the small beds. When the temperature has risen to about 120° F. about three days after making, it is advisable to thrust into the bed at intervals a stout iron bar such as is used for testing the temperature of hay stacks. The bar should be thrust in from the top of the bed to a depth of 21 inches, making the holes 12 inches apart.

In the ordinary way water vapour generated within the heap rises to the top and condenses near the surface, thus rendering the compost too wet. The holes described above assist the vapour to leave the bed and prevent the top layer from becoming too wet. They also let the heat escape and so prevent the bed from drying at the centre.

After making the beds and waiting for spawning it is necessary to protect them from unfavourable weather conditions such as a sudden down-pour of rain, which would make them too wet. This is done by covering lightly with a layer of straw, preferably barley straw, some 4 inches thick. This not only keeps the rain from the bed, but it also prevents the surface from drying.

After spawning, the straw covering which has been removed during the process must be replaced until the beds have been cased.

It is removed for casing and then the beds are protected finally with straw and mats or other material.

A layer of straw 6 to 12 inches deep is placed in

PLATE VII.

SPAWNING A FLAT BED.

[Facing p. 48

PLATE VIII.

Casing a Ridge Bed.

[*Facing p.*

Preparation, Spawning, and Casing

position all over the cased beds. Six inches is sufficient in hot weather but 12 inches of straw is required during cold weather, and up to 18 inches if very cold.

Finally the beds are covered with St. Petersburg mats, rush mats, or heavy sacking. If preferred, mats can be laid over the beds and held in position by lengths of hessian. This should be bound and fitted with rings through which a cord is passed for pegging down.

Mushrooms in Pastures and Lawns

Mushrooms can be grown with very little trouble in grassland of all kinds.

The method of spawning is simple. A square of turf 9 inches each way is pared off to a depth of 2 inches. Having removed this layer, a hole is dug out below to a depth of 9 inches. This hole is filled with prepared manure obtained in the following manner. A large barrow-load of clean strawy horse manure, free from sawdust or shavings is taken from the inside of a heap which had been stacked only for a short time. This is mixed thoroughly with about half a bushel of sifted loam taken from a depth of 1 to 7 inches below the turf. If soil is taken from the garden for this purpose the second spit should be used. If the mixture is dry it should be lightly watered by means of a watering can with a fine rose, leaving the mixture uniformly moist throughout the entire heap, after which it should be left for 24 hours under cover.

After filling the hole to within 1 inch of the surface, a piece of spawn is placed in the centre at a depth of 1 inch. The compost is then pressed down firmly, the turf is replaced, and the surface firmed by patting

The Cultivation of Mushrooms

with the back of a spade. Twelve inches should be left between any two adjacent holes.

If an easier method is required holes can be made in the turf to a depth of 4 or 5 inches, spacing them 18 inches apart in every direction and inserting in each hole a handful of manure in the centre of which is placed a piece of spawn. The turf should be replaced and patted down firmly with the back of a spade. A turf cutter such as is used for making the holes in a golf green is a useful tool for this work.

A light dressing of agricultural salt using 5 to 7 cwts. per acre during showery weather and just before the mushrooms are due will be found of benefit. If there is danger of early Autumn frosts finishing the crop, a light covering of straw litter over the spawned area will often prolong it.

Spawning

After the beds have been made the temperature gradually rises until 110° F. to 130° F. is reached. Naturally this temperature is highest in a ridge bed, lower in a double small ridge bed, and lowest in a flat bed. If this does not happen something is wrong, and in bad cases drastic measures must be adopted. Should the bed not commence to heat in two days from the time of making, a 6 in. covering of straw litter may have the desired effect.

After attaining this height the temperature steadily falls, and must be carefully watched to seize the right moment for spawning. The ideal temperature of the compost for spawning is accepted as 70° F. but it is safe to spawn at 80° F. If the temperature is falling rapidly and is, say, 100° F. one day, 90° F. the next,

Preparation, Spawning, and Casing

and 80° F. the next it is best to spawn at 80° F., but if the temperature falls more gradually, as it usually does, it is best to spawn at 70° F. or at most a few degrees higher. The temperature of the house must be kept at 60° F. to 65° F. for the first fortnight after spawning, reducing it gradually to 52° F. to 55° F. The paths must be damped once each day to create a moist atmosphere. This treatment encourages a rapid and abundant growth of mycelium and is the foundation for a good crop.

With the advent of pure culture spawn the size of the portion to be inserted at each spot is less than it was in the days of brick spawn. All that is required is a piece about the size of a large walnut. Pieces of spawn are inserted into the manure every 9 or 10 inches, and the rows should be staggered (Plate VII, facing page 48).

One carton of spawn is sufficient for 35-40 square feet of bed, dependent upon the size of the pieces used, when inserted 9 to 10 inches apart each way.

In spawning it is permissible to break the surface of the compost with a sharp piece of wood and finish the job with the fingers. A hole some 2 inches deep is opened up, and the spawn inserted so that it will be covered with not more than an inch of compost. It is important here to see that the compost is tucked in closely round the piece of spawn so that the mycelium will come into immediate contact with it when it grows away from the spawn. Cavities near the spawn are detrimental to good growth of the mycelium. Finally the compost is filled in over the spawn and the surface levelled and firmed with the hand.

After spawning, the mycelium or fungus threads will

commence to "run" into the compost and the growth can usually be seen between the fifth and seventh day. The mycelial growth is smoky grey in colour and consists of delicate threads permeating the compost. If the threads become white and thick it suggests that something is wrong. After a time the mycelium grows out at the surface of the bed as a white circular plaque and when this is well developed the time for casing has arrived. This may take fourteen to twenty-one days under good conditions. Premature casing is incorrect, because if the spawn has not grown sufficiently into the compost its growth is checked by the application of casing soil, which cools the surface and also cuts off the air supply to some extent.

Experiments at the Cheshunt Research Station were arranged so that beds were cased 7 days and 21 days after spawning. Isolated mushrooms appeared eight days earlier from the early cased beds than from the others, but the later beds produced typical clumps of mushrooms, and the final yield from the later cased beds was more than double that of the prematurely cased beds.

Should the surface of the bed appear to be dry it can be lightly damped occasionally. A can fitted with a very fine rose must be used and water applied by swishing the spray quickly over the bed.

CASING

Part of the investigations at the Cheshunt Research Station have been concerned with the influence of the material used for casing on the quality and weight of crop produced and they have proved extremely

Preparation, Spawning, and Casing

valuable.

It has been shown that certain diseases such as *Mycogyne* and the truffle fungus *Pseudobalsamia microspora* are introduced in casing soil and also that the casing material, apart from the transmission of disease, decides to some extent the quality and form of the mushrooms and and also the crop yield.

Thus soil taken from low ground which is apt to be wet and cold in the winter is extremely harmful. It causes the mushrooms to appear as isolated individuals, with long pithy stalks and poor quality cups. It reduces the yield to negligible proportions. Such soil when examined bacteriologically generally contains very few bacteria.

Also the texture of the soil is important, heavy soils tending to produce firmer and larger mushrooms with shorter stalks than soil of a sandy nature. The effect of casing material was illustrated admirably by a series of experiments in which various kinds of material were used for casing beds. These included sand, small stones, granite chips, and peat, both alone and mixed with an equal volume of sterilized soil. The crop yields at the end of ten weeks were given below.

Casing Material	Weight of crop in lb. per square foot
Granite chips	1·49
Sand	1·48
Stones	1·80
Peat	0·81
Sand and Soil	3·66
Stones and soil	3·13
Peat and soil	3·32
Soil only	2·45

The Cultivation of Mushrooms

Low yields were obtained from granite chips, sand, stones, and soil alone, but the addition of half sand, stones, and peat respectively increased the yield above that produced when the beds were cased with soil only.

It must be clearly borne in mind that these results are not finite. They were obtained from preliminary experiments and any grower who adopts any of the above mixtures on a large scale without first testing them on a few square feet of bed is unwise. They form a useful guide to future investigations and suggest that ordinary soil can be improved by adding such materials as will increase its water holding capacity and facilitate aeration.

Future work may show that soil with sand, stones, and peat, in proportions suitable for the particular type of soil used, may be more suitable for casing mushroom beds than soil alone.

For the guidance of growers who may wish to experiment for themselves the following mixtures are suggested:—

(1) Sterilized soil 3 parts, sphagnum peat 1 part.
(2) Sterilized soil 3 parts, stones 1 part.
(3) Sterilized soil, 2 parts, stones 1 part, peat 1 part.

The peat must be thoroughly wetted before mixing with the soil because it is difficult to wet dry peat when it is covering the beds.

Thus it seems that the selection of soil for casing requires a good deal of consideration if the best results are to be obtained. It should be taken from well drained land, well above the water table and never from areas which are very wet during the winter.

Where the soil is known to be free from diseases and pests, it need not be sterilized but in this case it should

Preparation, Spawning, and Casing

be taken from the second spit and be free from organic material.

Where there is any doubt concerning freedom from diseases, etc., the soil should be sterilized before use and can contain a little organic material.

A word of warning must be given about sterilized soil for casing. It should not be used too soon after sterilization because it usually contains an excess of ammonia which is considered to be injurious to mushroom spawn. Sterilization should have been carried out two or three months previously and certainly at least one month. It should be protected from possible re-contamination and should have been watered and turned several times.

Steam sterilized soil is preferred for casing but where it cannot be obtained virgin soil can be prepared in the following manner. Remove the turf from a field and dig out the next twelve or more inches of soil if suitable. It must be free from any obvious organic matter. Stack this in a ridge and thoroughly mix with it hydrated lime at the rate of half a bushel to the cubic yard. The best soil for casing is a medium loam, but either lighter or heavier material can be used provided its moisture content is suitable.

The next process is to transfer the prepared soil, sterilized or otherwise, to the site and water it from a can with a fine rose, gauging the quantity in accordance with the degree of dryness. When sufficiently moist for casing, it must bind when compressed in the hand, but is not so wet that it will adhere to the back of a polished spade used in casing. It must not be used during the same day that it has been watered.

An ideal soil will not require screening, but large

The Cultivation of Mushrooms

lumps are not desirable and it is often better to knock the soil about with a fork or the back of a shovel rather than screen it to a very fine condition. A screen with meshes 1 inch wide is usually sufficiently fine.

Before taking the casing soil into the house, the paths must be cleaned by removing any coarse organic matter such as pieces of compost, for this tends to encourage diseases and pests if present in the casing. The casing soil may then be taken into the house and placed on the path or on boards if preferred.

The casing of large ridge beds is a difficult task for a beginner but it is soon learned. When finished it should be $1\frac{1}{2}$ inches thick at the bottom of the bed being reduced gradually to a thickness of 1 inch on the top. A flat bed offers no difficulty. The prepared soil is merely lifted on to the surface of the bed, firmed, and smoothed over with the back of a polished shovel.

Small ridge beds are a little more difficult to case, but the beginner has most trouble at first with the bigger ridge beds which usually are made for outside work. The task is made easier by casing the sides in three horizontal layers starting nearest the ground. First a strip about 6 feet long is put along the bottom of the side to a height of about 12 inches. Above this is placed a second strip, slightly shorter, and about a foot wide. This is done on both sides and finally the ridge is capped. When casing a shovelful of casing soil is taken, gently turned and cast on to the side of the bed. Almost before it has come to rest the shovel is quickly turned round and the soil caught and firmly smoothed into position with the back of it, the movement of the shovel being upwards and slightly to the left or right in accordance with the direction of working.

Preparation, Spawning, and Casing

Once in position the casing is firmly patted with a smoothing motion. If the soil is in the right condition of wetness it will adhere to the bed and will not stick to the back of the shovel. The ease of casing depends to a great extent upon the dexterity acquired in quickly turning the shovel to catch and place the soil in position (Plate VIII, facing page 49). Care must be taken not to hit too hard and so knock the casing away from the other side of the bed. The work is facilitated by having two men working one on each side while a third brings the soil to them from outside the house.

If the beginner cannot get the knack quickly he can apply the following method for a time, but it should be given up as soon as possible for the method described above.

In this second method the casing soil is wheeled up to the side of the bed in a wheelbarrow, and then tipped out against the side of the bed, so that the heap comes half-way up it. By means of a clean shovel a cut is made downwards from the top of the heap, leaving a layer of soil $1\frac{1}{2}$ inches thick covering the side of the bed. The portion of the heap towards the path is pushed out and the layer against the bed is firmed and smoothed in position. It is then a fairly easy matter to take the remaining soil and case the top of the bed.

If the surface of the bed is a little on the dry side before casing and the casing soil is slightly damper than it should be, no watering is necessary, but if both the bed and the casing soil are on the dry side, the surface of the bed should be watered lightly about half an hour before casing.

CHAPTER V

CARE OF THE BEDS, PICKING, GRADING, AND PACKING

When casing has been complete it is best to withhold for a time all watering apart from damping the paths occasionally, but how often this is done must depend upon the state of the atmosphere. During a hot July damping may be necessary every day, but this is exceptional.

Assuming the temperature of the house is about 65° F., for the first fortnight and then falls gradually to 55° F., the mycelium of the mushroom will spread rapidly through the bed and mushrooms will begin to appear in from six to eight weeks after spawning. Usually just before the mushrooms are due a number of different kinds of fungi will often appear on the surface. These are mainly different species of the genus *Coprinus*, and while their appearance is by no means inevitable, it is usually taken as a sign that everything is satisfactory. Few, if any, of these fungi appear after the first mushrooms have been picked. They should be dug out if their point of origin is deep, and brushed off if they penetrate no deeper than the surface. In addition a white powdery fungal growth often appears on the surface of the casing soil, and to remove this the bed should be brushed twice between casing and picking. All such material should be burnt at once. The first

Care of the Beds

brushing is necessary about fourteen days after casing, and a hand broom slightly stiffer than the ordinary sweeping broom is satisfactory: a yard broom is too coarse for this work.

Usually an odd mushroom will appear here and there before the main crop shows. When this happens it is time to begin watering.

When watering, as little as possible should be given but it must be sufficient not only to damp the dry places, but also to make the whole surface uniformly moist. This means that the dry places require more water than the damper areas. The best plan is to damp the dry areas first and then water lightly the entire bed. It must be borne in mind that the moisture content of the compost should be sufficient to carry through the whole crop, and it is not permissible to water the surface of the casing so heavily that the water passes through and wets the manure. If it does it will probably shorten the life of the crop. Therefore, any damping must be planned to maintain the casing soil in a nice moist condition without being too wet. More mushroom crops are spoiled by over-watering than by under-watering.

If there is any doubt about the necessity for watering, it is best to damp over the dry places only and leave watering until next day, but induce a moist atmosphere by swishing water overhead into the air from a can fitted with a fine rose. It is, however, virtually important to see that the casing soil does not dry out when the tiny pin-heads are just forming for the first flush. Over dryness at this stage is a common fault.

The temperature, humidity, and freshness of the air have an important effect upon the crop, and a great

The Cultivation of Mushrooms

deal of investigation is required concerning these conditions. Generally speaking mushrooms thrive in a moist atmosphere but are adversely affected by excessive dampness. All that can be said at present is that both air that is very dry and that which is very wet is unfavourable.

An air temperature of 55° F. is probably the optimum. At 65° F. growth is accelerated and the stalks tend to be longer, but 70° F. is definitely too high. At lower temperatures growth is slower, but quality is good and the mushrooms are firm. A temperature of 50° F. is rather low for suitable growth, but at 55° F. development is satisfactory. Recent experiments at Cheshunt have been arranged in which electrically heated beds were kept at 70° F. in unheated chambers. Under such conditions the mushrooms form deeper in the bed than usual, and push up the casing soil as they emerge. They are not so clean as those which develop nearer the surface. After a time a little heat was applied to the air and when the air temperature exceeded 50° F. the mushrooms began to develop at the surface.

VENTILATION

Although the air of the house should be moist it must not be stagnant and a little ventilation is always advisable except during very cold periods. Draughts, however, must be excluded for their drying effect on the beds is injurious.

Failure of the crop on the bottom beds has been associated many times with an accumulation of carbon-dioxide near the floor of the house. The relationship is not fully understood, although the crops improved

Care of the Beds

when the gas was prevented from settling to the bottom by moving the air with fans. The evidence indicates that air movement is important.

PICKING

There are two methods of picking. In one the mushroom is twisted out of the bed (Plate IX, facing page 64), placed stalk downwards in the basket, and removed to the packing shed, where the stalks are shortened prior to grading and packing. The other method, which is the better because the mushrooms are not contaminated with soil and dust, consists of twisting the mushroom out of the bed with one hand, shortening the stalk with a knife held in the other, allowing the soiled end to fall directly into a box or other receptacle, and placing the trimmed mushroom in a clean basket, which is then taken to the packing shed as before.

A cheap cotton glove on the hand used for picking prevents the fingers from becoming stained and so assists in keeping the mushrooms unstained. This is most important with the white strains.

In sheds it is convenient for each man to have two baskets which can be hung from the side boards by hooks. The trimmed mushrooms are placed in one and the trimmings, stalks, etc., in the other.

In twisting the mushroom out of the bed, a portion of the stalk is left behind when picking from clumps. *These must be dug out as soon as possible and the holes filled with soil similar to that used in casing.* A heap of such soil is kept in readiness, a small quantity being carried about in a box by the worker concerned.

No fear may be felt that mushroom mycelium is

The Cultivation of Mushrooms

being wasted by digging out the stalks, for in the course of a week or so mushrooms will appear again in the same places. This applies mainly to clumps of mushrooms. Single mushrooms are often twisted out so cleanly that no stalk remains, and it is sufficient to fill up the hole and level the surface. Dead stalks must on no account be left in the beds, for they encourage diseases and pests. The stalks which have been removed cannot always be burnt at once. If not they should be taken outside to a spot some distance from the houses, placed in a heap, or suitable container, sprinkled with a 2 per cent solution of formaldehyde (1 pint 40 per cent formaldehyde in 49 pints water), and covered with sacks also damped with formaldehyde. Each time a further batch is added, the heaps should be sprinkled with formaldehyde and the sacks also. The heap should be carted away at frequent intervals and either buried or burned. Diseased or injured mushrooms should not be allowed to remain in the beds, they must be treated as the stalks. A good dusting of quicklime in and around the hole should be given before filling up with soil.

The first appearance of the mushroom crop in earnest usually takes the form of large clumps above the places where the pieces of spawn were introduced. Later the entire bed may become covered with single mushrooms and afterwards the crop appears in flushes at intervals of about ten days, unless something has happened to weaken the mycelium. The duration of the crop is from two to six months, the shortest crop occurring during the summer months, owing to atmospheric conditions. The normal crop averages between one to two pounds per square foot of bed surface. It

Care of the Beds

must not be thought that the bed can be left to take care of itself during the cropping period. Attention must be paid to watering as described previously. It is also a good plan to treat the beds once every seven to ten days with common salt, using a small tablespoonful to 2 gallons of water. It must be applied lightly from a can with a very fine rose, and appears to act as a fertilizer and helps to keep down pests to some extent. Picking must be carried out every day if possible, because if the mushrooms are allowed to open, their market value is reduced by half.

Grading and Picking

This, as with all forms of horticultural or agricultural produce, is most important, for upon the presentation successful marketing depends.

Mushrooms may be packed for market either in the salesman's own basket or in non-returnable baskets known to the industry as chips. It must be borne in mind, however, that diseases and pests may be carried from one nursery to another in returnable containers and for this reason, if for no other, non-returnable packages are preferable.

The following grading system was recommended by the Ministry of Agriculture for packing under the National Mark:—

Grade Designation.	Diameter of the cap.
Selected buttons	Not less than 1 in. or more than $1\frac{1}{2}$ in.
Selected cups	Not less than $1\frac{1}{2}$ in. or more than $2\frac{1}{2}$ in.
Selected cups (large)	Not less than $2\frac{1}{2}$ in. or more than $3\frac{1}{2}$ in.
Selected flats	Not less than 1 in. or more than $4\frac{1}{2}$ in.

The Cultivation of Mushrooms

During the process of grading and packing, particles of solid and dust adhering to the mushroom should be wiped off with a piece of dry flannel, or dusted off with a fine brush.

PLATE IX.

GATHERING THE CROP.

[Facing p. 64

A.—Mushroom attacked by *Mycogone perniciosa* in localized areas.

B.—Advanced stage of mycogone disease.

CHAPTER VI

DISEASES AND PESTS

There is no particular reason why clean crops of mushrooms should not be grown regularly provided good manure and clean soil are used and precautions to prevent infection and maintain clean conditions are taken, but the conditions of darkness under which mushrooms are grown are frequently allowed to obscure a lack of cleanliness both of the houses and the beds themselves.

A well kept mushroom house presents a delightful picture of orderliness and uniformity. Beds should be neat and well shaped, paths must be swept free from organic matter, all stumps must be removed immediately and the holes filled up with new casing soil, while the water tanks must be kept clean. Under such conditions, except by an unfortunate accident, diseases are unlikely to cause much damage, although the control of pests is still far from perfect. Untidiness and disorder are the certain precursors of trouble.

FUNGUS DISEASES

Mycogone

Mycogone or " bubbles " is a disease caused by the fungus *Mycogone perniciosa*. It has been recognized on the Continent for many generations and is probably the commonest mushroom disease. Although easily controlled it has been known to cause heavy losses.

The symptoms vary considerably. In slight attacks patches of white fungal growth appear on the gills in localized areas (Plate XA, facing page 65), and the shape of the mushroom is not changed to any extent. In bad cases the entire mushroom is much swollen, and becomes a round warty mass of grotesque appearance (Plate XB).

The stalk is greatly enlarged, the cap is almost indistinguishable and the whole structure is covered in a white fungal growth. Finally drops of watery exudate form on the surface and a bad odour is evolved.

Each diseased mushroom is a centre from which the disease may spread rapidly, for millions of spores are produced at the surface and these are readily distributed by insects, workers, tools, draughts, etc. As soon as a diseased mushroom appears it should be carefully dug out, taking away the entire stump and as much of the soil and compost as is necessary. It should be lifted carefully without undue shaking, laid in a paper lined receptacle placed close at hand, on the bed, and the whole burnt immediately. Care must be taken to impress upon the workers the ease with which the spores are shaken off and left on the bed to cause future damage. The hole left behind must be dusted thickly at once with hydrated lime and then filled up with new soil with which 20 per cent lime has been mixed. A little lime should also be dusted on the surface of the bed around the spot. Mycogone will not tolerate an excess of lime and can be controlled in this manner.

This disease is worst when the temperature is high and when the air is very moist and stagnant. Should the disease be serious, the air temperature should be reduced below 50° F. and the house allowed to dry

Diseases and Pests

out by withholding water and applying ventilation. Serious outbreaks can be prevented by keeping a sharp look-out for the first signs of the disease and dealing with it *at once*. It is claimed by some that the brown strains of mushrooms are more resistant than the white strains to this disease. Treschow[1] in Holland has controlled outbreaks by spraying the beds with Bordeaux mixture 1-1-50 at the rate of 1 litre per square metre.

Truffle

The truffle disease due to *Pseudobalsamia microspora* Diehl and Lambert (Plate XI, facing page 72) was first discovered in this country by Williams, who published an account of it in 1936[2]. It had already been reported by Diehl and Lambert[3] as occurring in mushroom beds in several parts of the United States, and since then has been found in Denmark, but never in Great Britain until July, 1936, when it occurred in the mushroom shed at the Cheshunt Research Station, being introduced in imported casing soil.

Pseudobalsamia is not parasitic on the mushroom itself, but is a competitor in the beds and under favourable conditions it fills the compost so quickly and to such an extent that for all practical purposes the mushroom crop ceases.

Development of the truffle generally commences near the surface of the compost forming a dense mat of mycelial threads in which the fruiting bodies or ascocarps are produced in abundance. The ascocarps

[1] " *Champignondyrkning i Haver* " C. Treschow, Friesia 3: 189-196, 1946.
[2] " A disease of mushrooms new to Great Britain," *Gardeners' Chronicle*. Vol. c, No. 2591, p. 147, 22nd August, 1936.
[3] W. W. Diehl and E. B. Lambert, *Mycologia*. Vol. xxii, p. 223, 1930.

are cream to reddish brown in colour, subspherical to discoid in shape, and are lobed. In size they vary from a diameter of ⅛ in. to that of 1 inch. Infection is carried in the casing soil and this may be the chief means of transmission.

Beds which are too wet and too tight favour this fungus at the expense of the mushroom, while high temperatures and poor ventilation also increase its rate of growth.

All attempts to destroy the infection in the experimental beds at Cheshunt in 1936 failed, and this fungus is regarded as a distinct menace to mushroom work.

Williams concluded from its habit of growing near the surface of the beds that *Pseudobalsamia* is not likely to be found in subsoil to any extent, but the damage of which it is capable emphasises the importance of sterilizing all soil used for casing purposes. Kligman[1] says that the spores survived for 3 hours at 200° F., but were killed by 20 minutes at 250° F. Ordinary sterlization may not eliminate this fungus from the soil. He says also that the fungus does not spread to any extent in the soil and severe outbreaks indicate that the soil was heavily contaminated before use. The fungus can be controlled by keeping the temperature down to 60° F. and infected parts of the bed can be dried out to kill the mycelium and then brought into bearing again by watering.

Flock or Gill Mould

A white fungus *Cephalosporium lamellæcola* occasionally attacks a few isolated mushrooms on a bed, but it

---

[1] "Control of the truffle in beds of the cultivated mushroom." Kligman, A. M., *Phytopathology*. 34: 376–384, 1944.

Diseases and Pests

need not be feared greatly because it rarely reaches serious proportions. As the name implies, it attacks the gills of the mushroom, binding them together with a white fungal growth (Plate XIIA). The cups and gills of infected mushrooms become very hard and stiff.

The disease is reputed to be favoured by high humidities and wetness of the casing soil.

Flock should not be confused with a genetic abnormality, Plate XIIB, in which the mushroom becomes extremely hard and tough and in which gill formation is so much retarded that each gill is represented by a ridge which is just perceptible. Where this abnormality occurs the percentage of mushrooms affected is usually so low that they are of no importance.

"*Damping off*"

The term "damping off" has been applied by Wood[1] to a disease of mushrooms in which they become brown and withered at all stages of growth.

Sometimes the young nodules are destroyed before they emerge above the casing soil, but usually the symptoms do not appear until the young buttons can be seen at the surface, when those which are infected turn brown and become pithy inside. In other cases, infection is revealed by the development of pithy mushrooms in which the stems are half-withered and brown inside.

Infection is contracted from the casing soil and is due to the presence of various species of Fusarium of

---

[1] Wood, F. C., "Studies on 'damping off' of cultivated mushrooms and its association with Fusarium species," *Phytopathology*. Vol. 27, No. 1, pp. 85–94, 1937.

which the commonest are *F. oxysporum* and *F. martii*.
Another source of infection seems to be the water supply and mushroom growers should be careful to use clean water for all their work. That from shallow surface wells, ponds, streams, etc., may be infected.

This disease emphasizes again the advantage of using sterilized soil for casing purposes. Similar symptoms may be caused by disturbance of the mycelium when picking.

" Cob-web " disease

A disease which has been called " cob-web " disease by some growers is caused by *Dactylium dendroides* of which the perfect form is *Hypomyces rosellus*,

This fungus forms a greyish white cottony growth over and around the individual mushrooms, frequently enveloping and destroying them completely (Plate XIII). Infection is often present on beds from which the old stem bases have not been removed immediately and if much of this material lies on the surface the disease may be serious. Excessive humidity and cold conditions favour attack by this fungus.

In his *Handbook of the Large Fungi*. 1923, Rambottom indicates that this fungus attacks the gills of several fungi, including *Stereum hirsutum. Cantharellus aurantiacus* and others. *Cantharellus* grows wild in woods and pastures, a fact which confirms observations in mushroom sheds which suggest the transmission of this disease in casing soil.

Spraying isolated spots with a 2% solution of formaldehyde (1 part 40% formaldehyde in 49 parts water) has been suggested as a control, but it is a

Diseases and Pests

drastic measure and *should be tested on a very small scale by anyone who wishes to try it.*

White Plaster Mould.—White plaster mould is a serious disease of mushroom beds, for although it first appears on the surface of the casing soil as a thin dense layer suggestive of a heavy dusting of flour it also travels deeply into the bed and permeates it to the detriment of the mushroom mycelium. If left uncontrolled it may cause complete failure of the crop.

The fungus concerned is *Scopulariopsis* (*Monilia*) *fimicola* and if the white floury growth is examined under the microscope it will be found to consist of thin threads and millions of tiny spores produced in chains. These spores are spread easily by draughts and by the ordinary cultural operations.

In 1936, Williams,[1] working at the Cheshunt Research Station, discovered that *S. fimicola* would not grow on acid potato agar, pH $2 \cdot 8$–$4 \cdot 6$, while there was a pronounced increase in growth as the medium was made more and more alkaline. This discovery lead to practical measures being evolved for controlling this disease.

Observations in mushroom sheds indicate that it is not easy to detect white plaster mould until about twelve days after casing, when the fungus appears as small white areas on the surface. Closer examination reveals the fact that the fungus has spread to a greater extent in the compost below. If the diameter of the surface colony is 2 inches the areas below the casing soil may be 6 inches or more in width.

[1] Williams, P. H., *22nd Annual Report, Experimental and Research Station*. Cheshunt.

The Cultivation of Mushrooms

It was found that the fungus could be prevented from spreading through the bed by removing the infected material and filling the hole with acid peat saturated with acetic acid.

After successful trials on many nurseries it is possible to give the following recommendations.

(1) Remove carefully the infected casing soil, placing it without spilling in a paper lined box, near at hand. Then remove the surrounding casing soil until the compost below is uncovered slightly beyond the white infected area.

(2) Remove the white infected compost and fill up gradually with acid peat, moistening it thoroughly with dilute acetic acid applied from a small syringe or similar instrument. The acid solution is prepared by adding one part of 33% acetic acid to seven parts of water by volume (1 quart in 2 gallons). Sufficient acid must be added as will run into and wet some of the compost below and surrounding the peat.

(3) Finally re-cover with fresh casing soil.

This treatment must be applied as soon as the first infection appears on the surface, because in this way the infection is checked before it has made headway, which it does with great rapidity. Further, early treatment reduces the amount of compost which must be removed. In our experiments a large handful of peat was sufficient to fill loosely the hole in the bed.

Where shelves are used and the holes are deep it is advisable to place double thicknesses of newspaper on the surface of the bed beneath to prevent any acid from dripping through and injuring the mushrooms.

The results indicated that the fungus does not grow again in the acid treated areas, but if the patch treated

PLATE XI.

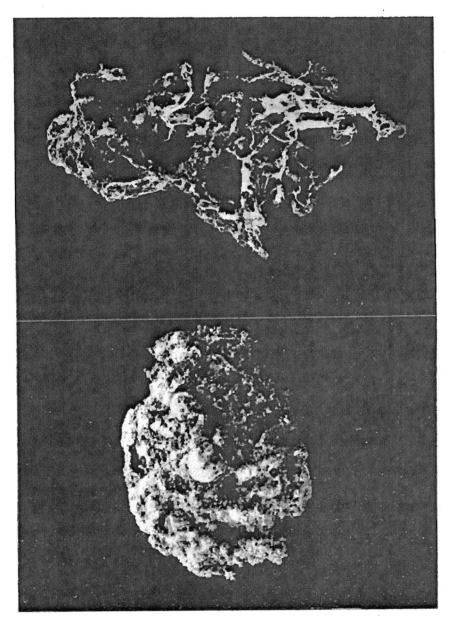

Pseudobalsamia microspora.

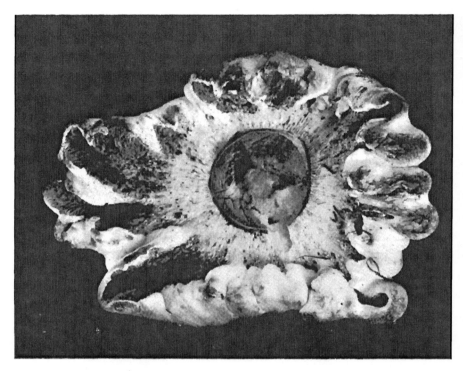

A.—Flock disease caused by *Cephalosporium lamellæcola*.

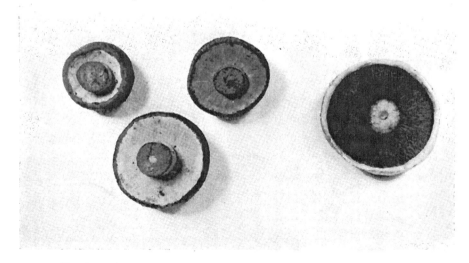

B.—Hard mushrooms with greatly reduced gills. Normal mushroom on right-hand side for comparison.

PLATE XIII.

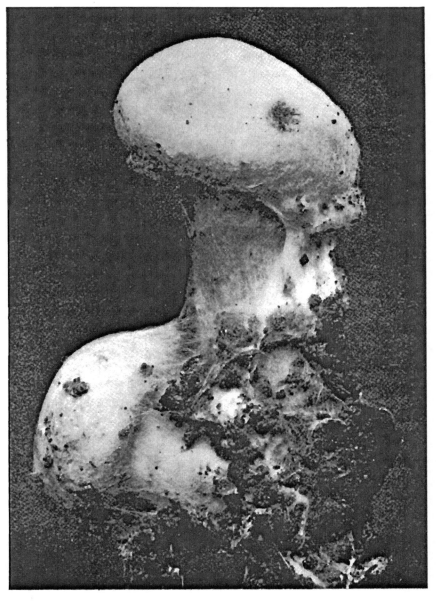

Cobweb disease, caused by *Dactylium dendroides*.

PLATE XIV.

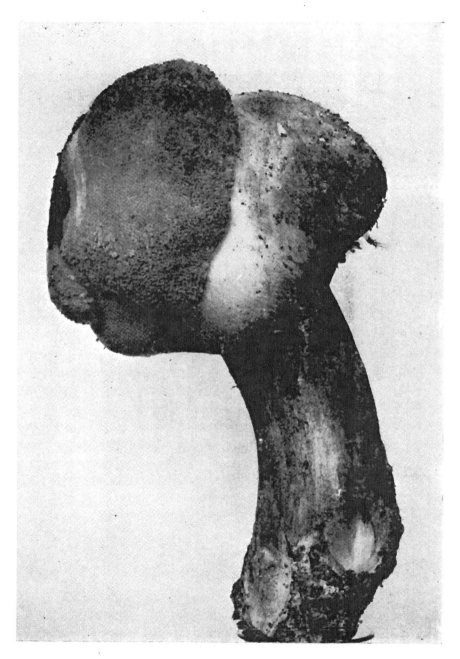

Rosecomb.

PLATE XV.

Mushroom attacked by *Verticillium malthousii*.

PLATE XVI.—*Mycetophilidae*

Sciara auripila Winn. Adult female. ×16.

Sciara auripila Winn. Adult male. ×16.

Eggs and young larva of *Sciara auripila* Winn. ×16.

Older larvae of *Sciara auripila* Winn. ×16.

Pupa of *Sciara auripila* Winn. ×16.

PLATE XVII.—*Phoridæ*

Megaselia halterata, Wood.
Adult female. × 16.

Megaselia halterata Wood.
Adult male. × 16.

Megaselia halterata Wood.
Pupa. × 16.

Megaselia halterata Wood.
Larva. × 16.

PLATE XVIII.—*Mushroom Mite*

Damage caused by Mushroom Mite.

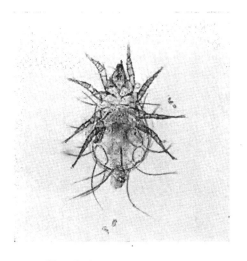

Tyroglyphus dimidiatus Herm.
Adult female. × 16.

Diseases and Pests

does not cover the whole of the infected area the fungus may grow again around the treated portion, and this must be treated again.

In one case *Scopulariopsis fimicola* developed in three large sheds containing six double shevles.

The first treatment occupied one man and a boy the whole of one day. The second treatment attending to new outbreaks five days later was finished by midday, and the third treatment required only two hours' work to complete. After this no further infection was seen.

The yield from these beds totalled 2½ lb. per square foot, and judging by recent experiences it would not have exceeded ½ lb. per square foot if the outbreak of *S. fimicola* had not been checked.

When treating ridge beds, it will be borne in mind that the acid tends to gravitate downwards, and therefore the sponge of peat holding the acid will be placed at the highest point of the areas to be treated.

Scopulariopsis fimicola can be seen growing occasionally on the manure during the process of turning especially if the material is too dry. In such cases the dry places should be thoroughly wetted with water and the heaps made higher than usual (about 6 feet) to encourage fermentation. The addition of gypsum also helps to prevent the development of this fungus. Badly infected heaps have been cleaned successfully in this way and any outbreaks in the beds checked with peat and acetic acid.

Contamination of the floor of the house, and also shelves where used, must be dealt with effectively, and this is discussed under the heading "Site Contamination," page 79.

The Cultivation of Mushrooms

Brown Plaster Mould

This fungus *Papulospora byssina* is neither so common nor so serious as white plaster mould for it is restricted usually to the surface of the casing soil. The patches are white and resemble plaster at the beginning but they soon assume a light brown and then a cinnamon-brown colour. If examined with a lens the growth is seen to be composed of tiny spherical bodies or bulbils.

Brown plaster mould has long been known in this country and was observed by the authors in 1919. The best treatment for infected beds is removal of the growth by scraping away the surface of the casing soil.

Cap blemishes

(*a*) *Spots.*—Spotting of the cap is frequently associated with the presence of various bacteria of which *Bacillus tolaasi* has been proved pathogenic. Work with most other bacteria has not yielded positive results and much of the spotting is still unexplained.

(*b*) *Blotches.*—Light and dark brown blotches are often traceable to the use of insecticides such as nicotine. Often they are unavoidable and the loss in commercial value must be included in the cost of pest control.

Occasionally an impure water supply has led to injury of this kind; the trouble has ceased on using pure drinking water.

Usually, however, large discoloured areas are caused by damping with water too late in the day and leaving the ventilators closed afterwards. Houses should always be ventilated after damping the beds until such time as the moisture has dried off the surface of the mushrooms.

Diseases and Pests

(c) *Cracking.*—Small cracks often develop on the caps, giving rise to a light and dark mottled appearance. This seems to be caused by severe variations in atmospheric humidity, and over-dryness. In sheds it can be prevented by sprinkling the paths when necessary, but in unsuitable buildings the maintenance of sufficient moisture in the air is difficult. Draughts must be avoided and sheets of Hessian may be hung around the walls and doors and damped each morning.

Rose Comb

Occasionally mushrooms develop a curious form of hypertrophy in which numerous swellings appear on the cap (Plate XIV). As these develop, they open and produce gills. The resemblance to rose comb of poultry seems to have suggested the name.

In 1930, Lambert[1] noted the connection between this malformation and the presence of certain fumes, especially those from coal-oil, and mineral oils, and the use of sprays containing pyrethrum and kerosene. His views are generally accepted and appear to be confirmed by observations in this country.

Verticillium malthousii

This fungus may attack cultivated mushrooms with the production of a white fungal growth on the gills and stalk (Plate XV). Infection is followed by browning and death of the mushroom attacked and the early stages of the disease are not unlike those of mycogone but the rate of decay is not so rapid.

It was described by Ware in 1933 from cases he had

---

[1] Lambert, E. B., " Two new diseases of cultivated mushrooms," *Phytopathology*. Vol. 20, No. 11, pp. 917–19.

seen during the course of his investigations.

Xylaria vaporaria

This fungus is a serious competitor of the mushroom in beds to which it has gained entrance. The white mycelium grows rapidly through the compost taking the food necessary for the growth of the mushroom mycelium. When the fungus invades the casing soil it produces its black, fleshy resting bodies or sclerotia. These vary in length from anything up to 6 or 7 inches, are frequently branched, and have an objectionable odour.

This disease is extremely difficult to control, and it seems useless to attempt to pull the sclerotia out of the soil, because the real damage is caused by the mycelium in the compost.

The source of the fungus is not obvious although the casing soil is suspected.

ANIMAL PESTS

Of the several animal pests with which the mushroom grower may have to contend, the most important are certain fungus-gnats (Mycetophilidæ known as Sciarid flies) (Plate XVI). They measure $\frac{1}{16}$ to $\frac{1}{8}$ in. in length, are slender and vary in colour from light brown to black. They may, in general, be distinguished from other and non-injurious flies by their habit of running very actively over the surface of the casing soil and the wood-work of shelves, etc.

Though doubtless the grubs or chrysalids are sometimes introduced into the bed with the manure of which it is composed, it appears also likely that the adult flies are naturally present (even during the winter) in glasshouses which are used for mushroom culture.

Diseases and Pests

The probability of the larvæ being present in casing soil, especially that which contains a good deal of organic matter, must not be overlooked. When the beds are made and cased, the flies are at once attracted to the warm fermenting mass, and without delay lay their eggs in the casing soil.

The grubs of these flies are white, but with jet-black heads provided with powerful jaws. When fully grown, they attain a length of about ⅜ in. and turn to naked white chrysalids encased in a loose cocoon of soil.

The young grubs probably feed at first upon organic matter in the bed, but when older and present in large numbers, enter the stalks and caps of the mushrooms, which then become entirely " maggoty " in cases of severe infestation, which are frequent.

Phorid flies, Plate XVII, are also found in mushroom beds, chiefly during the summer. They are more active than the Sciarids and have shorter, thicker bodies. The larvæ are without black heads and are much thicker than those of the latter. Phorid flies usually lay their eggs at the base of the mushroom, and the larvæ on hatching tunnel up the stem into the cap.

Next in importance comes the Mushroom mite, the species most frequently met with being *Tyroglyphus dimidiatus* Herm. (= *longior* Gerv.).

This very small animal, about the size of a small pin's head when full-grown, is of a shining white appearance. Its extremely slow movements distinguish it from the larger and quickly moving mites nearly always present upon the beds: the latter are entirely predatory and may play quite an important part in checking outbreaks of injurious animals. It is practically certain that the *Tyroglyphus* mite is introduced in the straw from manure heaps which have not attained a high and even temperature through lack of care in turning, though there is an admitted possibility of the mites being carried by insects.

Under conditions favourable to them, the mites may permeate the manure of the entire bed, and migrate to the mushrooms, where they become packed between the gills. Sometimes they live in colonies upon the caps, upon which they cause large and deep brown wounds by their feeding (Plate XVIII).

A larger, very active pink mite with extremely long legs, *Eugamasus.* is sometimes found in large clusters upon the caps. When brushed off, no injury has been found, and it is doubtful if this mite is similar to species of Linopodes which cause severe injury to mushrooms in Canada and U.S.A.

Springtails (*Collembola*) make their appearance with great frequency upon mushroom beds, sometimes in such unbelievable numbers that the beds appear of a blue or purple colour, at least in large patches. These are very minute insects which have a habit of hopping. Their origin is quite obscure, for they will appear quite suddenly and again disappear for no apparent reason. Damage to the crop has been attributed to them, but in all instances so far examined, they have found their way into holes in cap and stem made by some other agency.

The grubs of certain " gall-midges " (*Cecidomyidæ*) occur in the compost below the casing soil. Minute red or pink grubs of *Mycophila* may to some extent feed upon the mycelium but any real injury from them is doubtful. Longer white grubs without black heads (cf. the Sciarid grub) belong to a midge known as

Diseases and Pests

Miastor, These are definitely injurious, and are of some interest as they have never been known to transform to the adult fly, and produce young grubs inside themselves by a process of budding. The grub can withstand desiccation, and it is possible that they could be introduced in some types of spawn.

GENERAL CONTROL MEASURES FOR DISEASES, PESTS, AND OTHER CONTAMINATIONS

1. *Site Contamination*

Wherever mushrooms are cultivated certain contaminations, the nature of which is still unknown, pass into the soil beneath, with the result that succeeding crops of mushrooms become smaller and smaller until their cultivation ceases to be profitable. Although this fact has been known for years, it is not being recognized as it should and in consequence yields on many nurseries are lower than they ought to be.

The following examples may be quoted to illustrate the danger from this type of contamination.

(*a*) *Beds on the floor of glasshouses.*—In one case where mushrooms had not been grown previously the yield from 8 in. flat beds was 2·5 lb. per square foot during the winter. Tomatoes were grown during the summer and new flat beds put down in September for a second mushroom crop. The yield amounted to 1·2 lb. per square foot and during the next two winters it did not reach 1 lb. per square foot although in an adjacent block where mushrooms were being grown for the first time it averaged 2·2 lb. per square foot.

(*b*) *Ridge beds in the open.*—A farmer in the south of

The Cultivation of Mushrooms

England started the cultivation of mushrooms in standard ridge beds and obtained a yield of 1·9 lb. per square foot during the first crop. The following year, new beds were constructed on the old site and also on an equal area in an adjoining field. The yield was 1 lb. per square foot on the old site and 1·8 lb. per square foot on the new site. Next year these sites were covered with new beds and a new site also taken over in the normal extension of the work. The beds on the oldest site were a complete failure. They cropped for a few weeks and yielded less than 0·5 lb. per square foot. On the second year site the yield was 0·8 lb. per square foot, but in the new site it was 1·8 lb. per square foot.

As the years passed, these results were repeated again and the grower was compelled to transfer the mushroom work to another farm.

(c) *Beds on the floor in wooden sheds.*—On the nursery of Mr. Harnett a new mushroom shed of the old type was built for 1932, and beds of the double ridge type were used.

The yields per square foot in succeeding years were as follows:—

	lb. per square foot.
1932	2·3
1932	0·5
1933	2·5
1933	2·4
1934	2·0
1934	2·5

After the failure of the second crop in 1932, plans were made to counteract the injurious effect of the base and being careful they were repeated before each new crop.

Diseases and Pests

The site was scraped, swept clean, treated with sufficient formaldehyde to saturate the top 3 inches dusted with lime and covered with a layer of clean soil 2 inches deep.

The result can be seen from the table on page 80. Cases similar to the above are typical of what has happened in the mushroom industry and are a clear indication of the importance of the problem.

Proof that contaminated soil can be picked up and mixed with the manure has been obtained as follows:—

In an experiment the floor was covered with a layer of hydrated lime about $\frac{1}{4}$ in. thick and over it was spread a 2 in. layer of clean subsoil from an adjoining field. This was compacted by treading and the manure compost was brought in for the last two turns prior to bed making. When the beds had been made, the lime could be seen plainly in the ground beneath, showing that the top 2 inches of soil had been picked up unknowingly by the men and mixed with the compost. In this case the soil was new material and the crop was not injured in any way: the yield was 2·5 lb. per square foot.

Treatment

When ridge beds are made in the open it is easy to change the site and any expensive treatment of the ground may not be justified. It is, however, possible to renew the site each year by cleaning mechanically, treating with formaldehyde, covering the ground rather wider than the actual base of the beds with 2-3 inches of new soil.

The Cultivation of Mushrooms

In glasshouses, however, it is essential to clean the site before each new crop. Steam sterilization has not proved satisfactory and although the reason is not fully understood it may be connected with the production of ammonia or some of its derivatives.

The best treatment known so far is mechanical cleaning, and sterilization of the site with formaldehyde. For this purpose 1 gallon of 40% formaldehyde is mixed with 49 gallons of water and applied to 60 square yards for the purpose of saturating the top 3 inches of soil. Five to seven days later a covering of clean subsoil is placed over the site to a depth of 2 inches and after consolidating it, the compost is brought in and the beds made in the usual manner. This treatment has proved effective whenever it has been tried.

2. *Cleaning and disinfection of houses, sheds, etc.*

In mushroom work, extreme cleanliness is essential. Some growers may consider that the methods to be recommended are much too expensive but experience has shown, only too clearly, that they are necessary to success.

When the crop is finished the first task is to destroy as many insects as possible by the process of cyaniding, because any pests taken outside will continue to breed and will re-enter the houses when the next crop is developing. This is done by fumigating the houses with hydrogen cyanide and the most convenient method of doing this is to use proprietary cyaniding preparations which gives off the gas when exposed to air and moisture.

Diseases and Pests

The cubic capacity of the building is calculated by measuring in feet the length, width, height to the eaves and height to the ridge. The average height is obtained by adding the height of the ridge to the height of the eaves and dividing by two. The cubic capacity is obtained by multiplying the length by the width and the product by the average height.

$$\text{Average height} = \frac{\text{height to eaves} + \text{height to ridge}}{2}$$

Cubic capacity = length × width × average height.

Having calculated the cubic capacity of the house the necessary amount of the proprietary cyaniding powder, as advised by the manufacturer, should be sprinkled on the pathways of the houses.

This must be done by a responsible person and the houses locked until the following morning when they should be opened and thoroughly aired before anyone enters, for hydrogen cyanide is extremely poisonous to man. *For this reason it must not be used in buildings which adjoin or form part of any human habitation.*

If any serious disease has occurred in the beds, they should be soaked thoroughly with formaldehyde (1 gallon 40% formaldehyde in 49 gallons water) before removal, to prevent infection spreading outside, but when disease is absent, the beds can be taken out and stacked in some remote part of the nursery. When the mycelium is dead, the spent material may be used on certain crops, although for others it should be sterilized first. Expert advice should be sought before using it.

The next step is to sweep the houses, shelves, etc., clean and then thoroughly soak everything with formal-

The Cultivation of Mushrooms

dehyde, finally shutting up the houses and maintaining a temperature of 90° F. if possible for 48 hours. Afterwards the houses should be ventilated and washed down thoroughly when the vapours have escaped.

In ordinary houses, where beds are to be made on the soil floor, this should be treated for site contamination. In the case of shelves, the blow lamp must be used.

Too much emphasis cannot be laid upon the benefit which results from the blow lamp treatment, because in many cases it has been the means of growing successful crops after a series of failures. Every grower who specializes in shelf beds cannot afford to be without one or more blow lamps. For a preliminary trial, a painter's blow lamp may be used but the work is slow and larger instruments are now available.

The flame is moved quickly over the wood of the shelves and uprights so that any projecting fibres are singed but the surface of the timber is not burnt.

Some growers may wonder why the blow lamp must be used when so much care has been taken in applying formaldehyde, but until the nature of the contamination is fully understood an answer cannot be given. Experiments have shown, however, that the blow lamp treatment cannot be omitted.

3. *Fumigation at peak heat*

One great advantage of the shelf system is that the moisture content of the compost can be reduced if necessary by increasing the temperature of the shed before the beds have been compacted, and also that many of the insects present can be driven to the surface and destroyed by fumigation.

Diseases and Pests

When the compost is first placed on the shelves loosely it is about 14 inches deep, for this amount will ultimately compress down to 8 inches. After the house is closed down the temperature is gradually increased up to 90° F. If the compost is very wet the ventilators can be left open for a day or two until it has dried out sufficiently. Then the house is closed down and the temperature of the compost rises to 125°–130° F. When the temperature remains constant for two consecutive days "peak heat" has been reached, many flies have hatched out and most living creatures have come to the surface of the beds.

The shed is then fumigated with cyanide as described in connection with the cleaning and disinfection of houses. Next day the houses are opened to eliminate the poisonous gas before anyone is allowed to enter unless supplied with a suitable gas-mask.

4. *Pest control during the growing season.*

It is essential that control measures should be applied immediately the presence of a pest is observed since it is exceedingly difficult to eliminate several of the most serious pests of mushrooms once the beds have become invaded.

Regular dusting with DDT or pyrethrum dusts or treatment with DDT aerosols or smoke generators will destroy adult Sciarid flies. The larvæ within the beds are not destroyed by this treatment consequently if the beds become infested with larvæ it is necessary to treat them with nicotine solution.

For this purpose 10–15 fluid ounces of commercial

The Cultivation of Mushrooms

(95–98%) nicotine to every 100 gallons of water is recommended.

The day before the nicotine is to be applied the beds should be watered lightly with a solution of common salt (small tablespoon to 2 gallons of water). This brings many larvæ etc., to the surface and exposes them to the nicotine solution.

The nicotine is watered or sprayed carefully over the beds to wet the casing soil only. This treatment may be supplemented by trapping the adult flies upon white paper or pieces of glass smeared with a strong adhesive such as tangle-foot.

The flies are also attracted by light. If windows are present they can be uncovered for an hour each day, and cotton wool soaked in nicotine solution placed on the sills. The flies go to the windows and are killed by the nicotine fumes. Alternatively powerful lights may be installed in the shed and trays of paraffin or weak nicotine solution placed beneath to trap the flies.

The Mushroom mite *Tyroglyphus dimidiatus* is not easy to control. Where the mites exist at the surface of the beds they can be destroyed by means of a painter's blow-lamp, because, if carefully used, the surface can be burnt without injury to the mycelium below. This treatment has proved successful in many serious attacks and obviously it must be applied between flushes when only a few mushrooms exist here and there.

Pure grade 16 naphthalene can be used effectively, scattering it on the paths only at the rate of 4 oz. per 1,000 cubic feet. It should be applied between flushes, because the mushrooms may absorb some slight flavour, and they may also be disfigured by brown patches. By choosing the correct time, however, the

Diseases and Pests

maximum killing effect can be obtained with a minimum of damage. The treatment is one which can be recommended.

Woodlice may be trapped in pots and boxes containing hay, which are laid on the surface of the beds. Mangels, cut in half with the cut surface laid against the sides of the beds, are also useful traps.

Woodlice may be controlled by dusting the beds and paths of the house with DDT dusts.

Regular treatment of the beds with dilute salt solution is a valuable method for keeping the cultures healthy. It stimulates growth and seems to keep down diseases and pests. If the timber of boards and uprights are sawn, they should be treated by painting or spraying the surface with a good brand of creosote for it will soak into the timber and acts as a deterrant to flies of all kinds and does not harm the mushrooms. Planed wood is not suitable for the creosote does not soak in and the surface remains wet for a considerable time. This treatment has been highly effective at Cheshunt since 1937.

5. *General hygiene*

Those who contemplate the cultivation of mushrooms would be well advised to take full heed of the disastrous effect of contaminations of every kind, to study their natures so far as they are known and to learn the sources from which they are likely to arise.

The first essential is a clean start. Those who are sufficiently fortunate in possessing one of the latest sheds will have no difficulty in starting each crop under

The Cultivation of Mushrooms

clean conditions if they will follow the recommendations outlined previously. In the case of glasshouses and improvised structures over a soil floor the inside of the superstructure can be cleaned effectively but the soil is a breeding-ground for insects and also carries site contaminations unless treated suitably.

The compost itself may contain harmful insects and fungi unless it has been thoroughly fermented at the correct temperatures.

The casing soil, once disregarded as a source of diseases and pests, has proved an important source of infection. The use of sterilized soil eliminates this source of contamination and is preferred.

The water supply can also be a source of infection and must be taken into serious consideration. Clean, deep wells, or company's water of drinking quality should be used whenever possible. All water tanks should be thoroughly cleansed by scrubbing and treatment with formaldehyde.

Contamination can also be introduced by the workers from infected areas, on shoes, barrows, tools, etc. *No one should be allowed to stand on the side-boards of the bottom shelves to inspect the top shelves.* Disease has been carried in this way.

Expert advice should be sought immediately a pest or disease attack commences, unless the grower is conversant with the trouble and the methods adopted for controlling it. Diseases and pests which defy control when they have become well established can often be controlled quite easily at the commencement of an attack.

Brown plaster mould and other superficial growths can be checked readily by careful and regular brushing

Diseases and Pests

of the surface of the casing soil. They should not be allowed to accumulate. All diseased and broken mushrooms and stalks must be removed at once and the holes filled up with new casing soil, to which lime is added if the nature of the disease demands it. If this is not done, they form excellent breeding centres from which diseases and pests will spread rapidly. Care must be taken not to drop any infected pieces either in the beds or paths. They must be taken away at once and either soaked in formaldehyde or burned. Cleanliness outside the houses is equally important, and applies to fields of ridge beds or any form of culture.

When a serious disease develops in a portion of a bed, it is often advisable to soak it with a 2 per cent solution of emulsified cresylic acid prior to removing it for sterilization or destruction outside, because in some cases it is best to sacrifice a portion of the crop to save the remainder.

It must be remembered that mushroom diseases are encouraged by high temperatures and excessive dampness, and in consequence these should be avoided.

Conclusion

While the cultivation of mushrooms cannot be regarded as a carefree process there is no reason why it should not become a good source of income provided careful attention is paid to all the essential details. The scientific principles which underlie it are still not fully understood but when the knowledge has been wrested from Nature the maximum crops of to-day will no doubt become the average of to-morrow.

CHAPTER VII

COOKING RECIPES

The following recipes were supplied by the Editor of *Good Housekeeping* who has very kindly given permission for them to be included in this book. They have been extracted from *Good Housekeeping Fruit and Vegetable Cookery* and *The A B C of Cooking*,

To prepare mushrooms.—Peel the caps. This is done most readily when the mushrooms are fresh. Cut the ends off the stalks and scrape the stems. These may be removed entirely, if preferred, as they take longer to cook than the flesh. Chopped finely, mushrooms can be used for flavouring other dishes, such as stews and soups. Over-cooking makes them hard, and " over-seasoning " destroys their delicate flavour. Mushrooms, fried or grilled, shrink appreciably, and due allowance must be made for this fact when catering.

MUSHROOM PIE

1 *lb. mushrooms*   *A large stalk of celery*
¼ *lb. fat bacon*   *Lemon juice*
2 *tablespoonfuls water*   *Salt and pepper*
           ½ *lb. short or flaky pastry*

Prepare mushrooms and remove stalks, cutting up if large. Cut bacon in small pieces and chop celery finely. Fill a pie-dish with alternate layers of bacon and mushrooms, seasoning each well and sprinkling with lemon juice and celery. Then add the water, cover with the pastry, and bake in a quick oven for 20 minutes. Test the mushrooms with a skewer. If they are not cooked, cover the pastry with greased paper and move the pie to a cooler part of the oven until ready.

STUFFED MUSHROOMS

6 *croûtes fried bread*
6 *large mushrooms*
1 *heaped tablespoonful breadcrumbs*
1 *heaped teaspoonful grated cheese*
½ *teaspoonful chopped parsley*
Garlic

½ *oz. butter*
Salt and pepper
A little milk
Browned crumbs
Fried parsley

Prepare the mushrooms, which should be trimmed to an even size and good shape. Chop the stalks and trimmings finely. Cut the garlic and rub round the pan used for making the stuffing. Melt the butter in the pan, add all the ingredients except the croûtes and mushrooms and cook slowly until the breadcrumbs are well swollen, adding sufficient milk to make the mixture bind; it must not be wet. Put the mushrooms on a greased tin, pile the stuffing on neatly, and sprinkle with breadcrumbs. Cover the tin with greased paper and bake very gently in a moderate oven for 10 to 15 minutes. Have ready the croûtes of bread, which should be slightly smaller than the mushrooms. Serve the mushrooms on the croûtes, garnished with fried parsley.

CASSEROLE OF MUSHROOMS

¾ *lb. mushrooms*
3 *tomatoes*
1 *onion*
4 *tablespoonfuls water or stock*
1 *oz. fat*

Salt and pepper
1 *tablespoonful chopped parsley*
1 *sheep's kidney*

Cooking Recipes

Grease a casserole or pie-dish. Prepare the mushrooms and either use or remove the stalks according to preference. Skin the tomatoes, cut the onion into rings and fry in the fat to a golden brown. Cut the kidney into small pieces and fill up the dish with alternate layers of the ingredients. Season each layer well, sprinkle on a little parsley and finish with a layer of mushrooms on the top. Add the water, cover and stew gently until the mushrooms are tender. This will take 30 minutes in a moderate oven. The dish may be made in individual casseroles if preferred.

SCALLOPED MUSHROOMS

½ *lb. mushrooms*   *Grating of nutmeg*
1 *oz. fat*   *Salt and pper*
1 *oz. flour*   *Browned crumbs*
½ *pint milk*   *Chopped parsley*
1 *tomato*   *Coralline pepper*
               1 *hard-boiled egg*

Prepare the mushrooms, and cut them and the stems into pieces, roughly ¾ in. square. Make a white sauce with the flour, fat, and milk. Put in the mushrooms, season, and simmer gently 15–20 minutes or until the mushrooms are tender. Stir occasionally, and 10 minutes before the mixture is ready add the sliced egg and tomato. Have ready hot greased scollop shells or a pie-dish, pour the mixture in, sprinkle with hot brown crumbs and garnish alternatively individual dishes with chopped parsley and coralline pepper. Serve very hot.

The Cultivation of Mushrooms

Sole aux Champignons

1 filleted sole	A squeeze of lemon juice
½ lb. button mushrooms	1 teaspoonful chopped parsley
1 oz. butter	
	Salt and pepper

For the Sauce

Pint liquor and milk mixed	½ oz. flour
	½ oz. butter
	Anchovy essence

Roll the fillets round the thumb, skinned side inside, and place in a buttered tin. Skin the mushrooms, stew for 5 minutes with the lemon juice, parsley, seasoning, and butter. Keep a few mushrooms for a garnish. Fill the hollow fillets with the mixture, cover with greased paper and bake in a moderate oven for 20 minutes. Remove the fillets on to a dish, strain the liquor and make up to ¼ pint with melted butter. Melt the ½ oz. butter, add flour, then milk by degrees. Stir and boil for 8 minutes, colour a faint pink with anchovy sauce. Coat the fillets with the sauce, put a mushroom on the top of each and garnish with lemon butterflies.

Casserole of Rabbit with Mushrooms

1 rabbit	1 teaspoonful pepper
½ lb. mushrooms	1 small carrot
2 oz. flour	Water or stock
2 oz. dripping or butter	Red currant jelly
1 medium onion	2 teaspoonfuls salt

Wash the rabbit and soak in water for half an hour to draw out the blood. Wipe thoroughly and joint.

Cooking Recipes

Mix the flour and seasoning together and dip the joints in the seasoned flour. Heat the dripping until a faint blue smoke rises from it. Cut the onion into thin rings, fry until golden brown, remove and sauté the joints. Just cover the rabbit with water or stock. Add the thin rings of carrot together with the mushrooms peeled and chopped. Bake at 380° F. for 1½ hours. Serve with red currant jelly.

MUSHROOMS AND MACARONI

½ lb. prepared mushrooms   Salt and cayenne pepper
1 oz. butter   2 oz. macaroni
½ gill milk   2 oz. grated cheese
½ pint white sauce

Prepare the mushrooms, sauté them in butter, add the milk and stew until tender. Cook the macaroni in boiling salted water, add to it the white sauce together with the mushrooms, seasoning, and half the cheese. Turn into a buttered *gratin* dish, sprinkle the rest of the cheese on the top and bake at 400° F. until brown.

CALVES' LIVER WITH MUSHROOMS

3 oz. fat bacon   ¼ lb. mushrooms
½ lb. calves' liver   ½ pint water or stock
¼ head of cauliflower   Seasoned flour
Triangles of toast

Fry the bacon and keep it hot. Cut the liver into half-inch slices, wash well and dry. Dip it in the seasoned flour and fry in the bacon fat. Remove from the pan and fry the chopped mushrooms, then remove

The Cultivation of Mushrooms

these from the pan. Fry any remaining flour and add the water or stock. Stir and boil for 5 minutes. Add the bacon, liver, and mushrooms. Reheat and serve. Garnish with the cooked cauliflower head and triangles of toast.

SPINACH AND MUSHROOM CREAM

2 *lb. spinach*   1 *oz. butter*
1 *gill of white sauce* 1 *hard-boiled egg*
¼ *lb. mushrooms*   *Nutmeg*
            Salt and pepper

Prepare and boil the spinach as usual. Mash finely, arrange in a neat border and keep hot. Skin the mushrooms, chop, then sauté them in the butter. Add them to the white sauce together with a grating of nutmeg and seasoning. Reserve the yolk of egg for garnishing and add the chopped white to the sauce. Reheat and pour in the centre of the spinach border, then sieve the yolk of egg over.

MUSHROOM STEW

1 *lb. mushrooms*   ½ *oz. flour*
1½ *pints milk*   ½ *teaspoonful mace*
1 *oz. butter*   ½ *teaspoonful celery salt*
            Pepper and salt

Peel the mushrooms and cut in cubes. Add to the milk and bring to the boil. Melt the butter, add the flour and seasoning, make into a sauce with milk from mushrooms, return to mushrooms, allow to cook 15 minutes, stirring frequently. Serve with toast.

Cooking Recipes

Mushroom Savoury

1 *lb. mushrooms*
4 *medium tomatoes*
4 *heaped tablespoonfuls bread-crumbs*
1 *onion*
1 *teaspoonful grated lemon rind*
Salt and pepper
Croûtons of fried bread

Prepare the mushrooms, skin and slice the tomatoes, fry the onion rings in a little dripping or butter. Butter a *gratin* dish and arrange the mushrooms, tomatoes, crumbs, and onion in layers. Season each layer and sprinkle with lemon rind. Cover with greased paper and bake at 360° F. for three-quarters of an hour or until the mushrooms are tender. Garnish with croûtons of fried bread.

Mushroom Patties

Puff or flaky pastry
½ *lb. mushrooms*
1 *gill white sauce*
1 *level teaspoonful grated cheese*
Salt and pepper

Stew the mushrooms in the white sauce, and season to taste. Prepare patty cases of pastry, fill with the mixture, and bake in an oven at 400°–450° F. for 20 minutes or until golden brown. Garnish with the grated cheese.

CPSIA information can be obtained at www.ICGtesting.com
Printed in the USA
LVOW060808070713
341709LV00001B/326/P